Praise for the Science of Reading in Action

"I have learned so much more from this than I ever did in college, and I am excited to put it all into practice!"
-Samantha S.

"I have spent HOURS compiling word lists that matched the phonetic skills I was targeting while using an OG approach… and here they ALL are ready done and ready to go! Doing a happy dance right now. Thank you!!!"
- Malinda E.

"Wins from the last few days include feeling relief while doing phonics warm ups. My kiddos did well with them and made me feel like we're laying a good foundation. I also feel like I have a much more clear idea of what things to do and which order to do them in when we need to fill in any reading gaps. I didn't really know what SOR was a week ago, but I'm loving it now! Finally something that makes sense, is scientifically based, and works alongside kids' brain development! No more muddled ideas of what terms mean, what order to teach phonics concepts, or feelings of, 'Am I doing this right??'"
-Ali L.

"My students thrived with sound mapping just in one day. I have a 2nd and 3rd grader who are beginning readers. The activity worked great."
- Kim L.

"I found your resources while searching for support for my struggling reader. He struggled with sight words in particular. We started orthographic mapping with his sight words in meaningful groups instead of the listed order we had in our curriculum. They truly "clicked" for him in a few short days of practice. The same words we had been working on all school year so far! I can watch as it helps words become more meaningful for him. He is very mathematically minded and loves to look for patterns. Honing in on this skill with words has been a taste of magic for us!"
- Bonnie K.

"My favorite takeaways are the handouts that help me teach more effectively and systematically. My teaching approach I'm sad to say before this was all over the place. When you know better you can do better."
- Monica F.

"My favorite takeaway has been this beautiful increase of confidence as I teach my littles! Being a new teacher, I am doing my all to give my students the best education and learning experience I can give. The additional shared resources have brought such fun to my classroom. I love seeing my students' minds learning when they don't even know it!"
- Courtney O.

To my mother, who dedicated her professional life to education and inspired me to do the same.

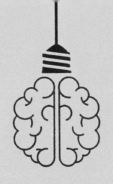

THE SCIENCE

OF READING

IN

ACTION

Brain-Friendly Strategies Every Teacher
Needs to Know

MALIA HOLLOWELL

The Science of Reading in Action

Published by TeacherGoals Publishing, LLC, Beech Grove, IN
www.teachergoals.com

Developmental and Copy Edits by My Writer's Connection

Cover and Interior Design by Amanda Fox

Illustrations by Simmi Patel

Paperback ISBN: 978-1-959419-02-0

Library of Congress Control Number: 2023930326

First Printing April 2023

Bulk purchases are great for your team of designers, teachers, or students.

TEACHERGOALS
PUBLISHING

Contents

1	Dear Reader
4	Chapter 1: Closing the Gap
16	Chapter 2: How Brains Really Learn to Read
42	Chapter 3: Phonological Awareness Isn't Just for Kindergarteners
66	Chapter 4: The Phonics Rules Every Child Needs to Learn
97	Chapter 5: How to Teach Words Ten Times Faster
113	Chapter 6: Are Sight Word Lists Dead?
121	Chapter 7: Building Powerhouse Language Comprehension
137	Chapter 8: Crossing the Finish Line to Comprehension
144	Chapter 9: Your Biggest Questions Answered
158	Chapter 10: What's Next?
162	Appendix A
166	Appendix B
167	References
192	About the Author
192	Professional Development
194	More from TeacherGoals Publishing

Dear Reader

If the first step to right teaching was doing it the wrong way, then I was ready to write this book years ago. Since walking into my first classroom back in 2003, I have experienced more failures than I can count: students who left my room reading below grade level, late nights spent worrying someone was slipping through the cracks, lesson plans I spent hours prepping only to have them flop.

What I now know is that many of the strategies and tools I used during those first few years of teaching have been proven to be ineffective and unhelpful. In some cases, research has shown those methods were even holding students back rather than helping them progress in their learning.

All of that failure drove me to become hyper-focused (Some might even call it obsessed!) with studying, testing, tweaking, and sharing the best research-based teaching strategies. My goal is to equip teachers like you to skip all the stress and worry and get right to the good stuff—helping your students become thriving readers.

In 2016, I created a four-week course called The Reading Roadmap. I wanted to make it easy for teachers to understand the reading research so they could implement better, more effective practices in their classrooms. The success stories that have come out of that training are profound. Participants walked away with greater confidence because they finally understood how to help all of their students achieve significant reading growth. The teachers were empowered by the knowledge and tools they had acquired in those four short weeks. They hit the ground running with the science of reading and experienced exciting teaching wins as a result. That training and the success stories that came out of it were the basis for this book.

I want you to experience that same kind of confidence and success, which is why I am so excited for you to join me on this learning journey. You have already taken the first step by picking up this book. Now comes the fun stuff!

Like teaching, this book is part art and part science. Teaching reading well requires both an understanding of how children's brains learn to read as well as the tools necessary to turn your knowledge into action. Have you ever left a teacher training excited to use what you've learned only to realize you have no idea how to implement any of that information? Me too; in fact, that's happened to me a lot through the years, and I am determined not to let history repeat itself.

The most important word in this book's title is Action. The Science of Reading in Action breaks down all of the must-know information and then goes one critical step further by giving you easy-to-implement strategies and techniques. I've filled these pages with actionable tools that you can use in your classroom immediately, from print-and-play activities to sanity-saving cheat sheets, classroom-tested teaching strategies, and more. It's all here because I know there is a difference between acquiring knowledge and understanding how to use it. I also know transformation is waiting for you—and your learners—on the other likely draw a blank. Imagine if a truck driver struggles to read the products on his invoice sheet or cannot log his mileage and travel history when he drives across the country. Picture a server floundering to write customers' breakfast orders because spelling is so difficult. Baseline literacy is a job requirement for nearly every profession in first-world countries. Without it, job seekers' opportunities are limited.

It is not surprising that in 2017, the United States Department of Education confirmed income is strongly related to literacy. Workers with the lowest literacy levels earned two times less than peers with highly proficient literacy even after controlling for factors including age, race, ethnicity, and parental education level.

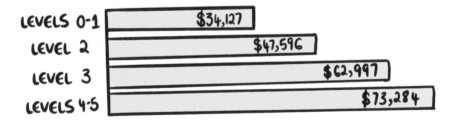

2017 AVERAGE INCOME BY READING LEVEL

AVG. YEARLY INCOME, 2020 USD

LEVELS 0-1	$34,127
LEVEL 2	$47,596
LEVEL 3	$62,997
LEVELS 4-5	$73,284

Unfortunately, low literacy also has generational impacts on student achievement. Research shows that a linguistically rich home environment is the most important contributing factor to children's early literacy and language development. When parents or caregivers read to children daily during their first five years of life, they can be exposed to 1.4 million more words than their kindergarten peers who experience minimal reading at home. As the Language Essentials for Teachers of Reading and Spelling (LETRS) describes, "Printed word recognition will be faster and more accurate if the spoken form of the word already exists in the person's listening vocabulary."

Children who start school with an abundant word bank have a launching pad they can use to successfully build reading skills, language comprehension, and academic success in other subjects, such as science and math. In contrast, kindergartners who come from homes where reading is not a daily habit (or a habit at all) have a smaller listening vocabulary—up to 1.4 million words fewer—which means they start school at a significant disadvantage compared with higher-literacy peers.

Literacy is not just a teaching issue; it is a social justice issue. Former United Nations' secretary-general Ban Ki-moon describes it as "a foundation for human rights, gender equality, and sustainable societies. It is essential to all our efforts to end extreme poverty and promote well-being for all people." Every child deserves the opportunity to learn how to read. It is critical that students receive the instruction and support they need at school to stop the generational cycle of low literacy once and for all.

When we add up the effects associated with low literacy levels, it is incredibly costly, not only for that person, but also for the global economy. The World Literacy Foundation calculates that it consumes more than $1.19 trillion annually.

The great news is that it does not have to be this way!

The Science of Reading in Action

Research shows that with the right tools and strategies, 95 percent of neurotypical students can learn to read by the end of first grade. That means you can be successful, your teaching partner can be successful, your school can be successful—we can all be successful—because students can learn to read. We just need to use proven, science-based strategies that empower learners for lifelong success. As the director of the Center for Dyslexia, Diverse Learners, and Social Justice at the University of California, Los Angeles (UCLA) highlights, the ripple effects of improved reading growth are tremendous. "Literacy changes our brains, which changes the life trajectory of a person, which changes society, which changes our species." Improved reading growth affects a student's individual life, but it also impacts their family and community for generations to come. We truly can improve the world one reader at a time.

Making the shift to science-based techniques may sound simple—and it can be—but often there's more going on in teachers' hearts and minds during this transition. I have spoken with thousands of teachers around the world and have noticed a few patterns that create roadblocks for educators.

Most teachers join the profession to make a positive difference in the world. They are wholeheartedly committed to the success of their students and take pride in doing their best every school day so that their class can reach its fullest potential. So when they realize, as I did, that the mandated literacy curriculums and teacher training they have relied on can actually prevent their students from succeeding, they feel betrayed and deceived. How could they have been led down the wrong path for so long? How could curriculums have reinforced harmful reading strategies for decades? Discovering that their lesson plans have been filled with ineffective tools and techniques can cause feelings of shame, embarrassment, and anxiety about what else they might have been doing wrong.

When humans experience stress or perceive danger, the brain sends a distress signal to the nervous system, triggering the fight-or-flight response. For some teachers, that response shows up as heightened emotions that impede their focus and may make them hesitant to try new approaches.

When I am training teachers, my first step is to make sure they understand that digging into the science of reading is not about pointing fingers, placing blame, or feeling guilty about past mistakes. That just keeps you stuck, and if you are stuck, so are your students. Learning the research is about failing forward and filling your teaching toolbox with the best, most effective teaching strategies so that you can help all of your students become thriving readers. My greatest hope is that these pages are not just a book; they are the foundation of a teaching movement.

The Reading Wars

Let's start by taking a quick look back at the history of reading instruction and examining what worked well and what did not. You may have heard the term the reading wars before—the ongoing disagreements and continually changing beliefs about how students learn to read. You've almost certainly experienced it. (When I began teaching in 2003, we referred to the phenomenon as the pendulum swing.)

The Science of Reading in Action

The modern-day reading wars began back in the 1950s when well-respected scholars such as William Gray encouraged teachers to skip isolated phonics drills in favor of having students memorize whole words—a method he called look–say. Gray claimed, "The old mechanical phonics drills . . . inevitably result in dull, word-by-word reading." He preferred having children learn full words so they could be more efficient and skip the sounding-out step completely.

In 1955, a scholar named Rudolf Flesch drew a deep line in the sand with his book Why Johnny Can't Read. He presented a strong phonics-first message and demanded that teachers help children connect letters to sounds so they learn how to blend those sounds and eventually read words. Flesch argued that teaching phonics consistently would empower students to make the connections necessary for reading increasingly difficult text.

For more than a decade, the two sides competed for acceptance. In 1967, Jeanne Chall, a professor at Harvard University's Graduate School of Education, provided a compelling verdict after analyzing findings from thirty different studies: 90 percent found that phonics-based programs resulted in superior reading outcomes for students. She concluded that teaching students the sounds that letters and letter combinations made was the key to unlocking their reading growth. Phonics should be king.

But a decade later, the education community saw a significant shift with yet another theory claiming the human brain could naturally learn how to read, just as it naturally learns to speak. A well-known psychology professor named Frank Smith suggested that teachers who are helping struggling readers should have them "skip over the puzzling word. The second alternative is to guess what the unknown word might be. And the final and least preferred alternative is to sound the word out. Phonics, in other words, comes last."

Despite research findings showing the strategy's ineffectiveness, the new curricula encouraged teachers to replace phonics lessons with "whole language" practice and simply put books in kids' hands so they could connect the dots on their own. Almost overnight, classrooms fell silent with independent reading time.

It wasn't until the NAEP released a fresh batch of reading score data in 1994 that whole language came under fire. California's fourth-grade scores fell significantly, and the state suddenly found itself near the bottom of education rankings. Most Californian teachers reported that they relied heavily on whole language methods in their classrooms, linking the approach to the decline in scores. Legislators in California and around the country passed phonics and phonemic awareness bills, hoping to improve student performance.

Three years later, the United States Congress tasked a group of fifteen literacy experts called the National Reading Panel (NRP) to identify the most effective teaching tools and strategies for reading instruction. The NRP published its findings in 2000, and among its conclusions was confirmation that teaching phonics, phonemic awareness, oral guided reading, and comprehension strategies were far more effective than silent reading, which provided children with no teacher feedback. Contrary to popular thought, teacher-directed instruction was critical to spurring students' reading growth.

And yet, despite the NRP report, the pendulum swung to an approach called "balanced literacy." Schools across the country adopted the combination of phonics and whole language, topped off with lessons teaching reading strategies such as looking at pictures for clues, skipping unfamiliar words, and flipping vowel sounds until arriving at a guess that makes sense. As the name suggests, balanced literacy was supposed to be the best of both camps—the magic formula for providing the must-have teaching components that would unlock students' reading growth. However, the balanced literacy approach ignored essential pieces of the puzzle, including phonemic awareness, while promoting unfounded reading strategies that favored guessing words instead of sounding them out.

Subsequent NAEP data shows that balanced literacy did not deliver on its promises. Students struggled. Without learning the letter–sound connections, phonemic awareness skills, and other necessary components of reading, many children continued to fall behind.

In 2018, Emily Hanford published an article in *The New York Times* criticizing balanced literacy. She pointed to the statistics on struggling readers and demanded that educators examine the decades of research pinpointing how brains learn to read. Neuroscientists, literacy experts, classroom teachers, and speech pathologists worldwide had spent decades identifying which teaching strategies and tools work and which do not. Hanford concluded, "There has been a huge amount of research, *thousands* of studies, and what was once a big mystery is now common knowledge among cognitive scientists, psychologists, and other researchers who study how people learn. But it's *not* common knowledge among teachers." The people who most needed the insights about best practices for teaching literacy—the teachers who were helping students learn to read every day—did not have easy access to it… Yet.

Educators, parents, and concerned politicians tweeted, forwarded, and shared Hanford's article far and wide, bringing the conversations about literacy and how teachers are prepared (or *not* prepared) to teach reading into mainstream media. Finally, the pendulum swing between phonics, whole language, and balanced literacy stopped in its tracks. The reading wars had come to an end. What replaced it? The science of reading.

The Science of Reading

Take a moment to imagine every case study, brain scan, and science journal that has been collected on reading during the past seventy years. If you were to compile all of that information in neatly organized stacks, it would easily fill a warehouse!

In one of those stacks, you'd find reports from neuroscientists who scanned children's brains before they could read, while they were learning to read, and then after they became fluent readers, so they could track shifts over time. They discovered that our brains undergo anatomical changes during the learning process, including the development of neural pathways that connect our visual system to spoken language and meaning-making regions. With this new superhighway in place, a child can see a word, pronounce it in their head, and then connect it to the appropriate meaning.

Another massive stack of reports might include findings from speech pathologists who explored how new readers connect spoken communication to written text. Among their findings was the discovery that students make faster letter–sound connections when they start with a speech sound rather than the written letter. Because children learn to speak before they learn to read, homing in on a speech sound's distinct look and feel before attaching it to the letters used to spell it enables them to take advantage of background knowledge they already have in place. They can move from something known to something new instead of the other way around.

The Science of Reading in Action

Countless other collections of data from other experts reach from floor to rafters in this cavernous warehouse. From the classroom teachers who tested strategies and tools to identify the methods that resulted in the biggest reading growth to the psychologists who explored how people make sense of text as they read, many people have contributed to the wealth of knowledge we call the science of reading.

Thanks to decades of collective research, the science of reading confidently pinpoints what works so you can continue doing it and, just as important, the data highlights what does not work so you can stop wasting your time. The value of this information is immeasurable. The struggle is synthesizing it and then implementing the most effective practices. That's where this book comes in. The science of reading, as comprehensive as it is, does not have to be overwhelming. Even better, you can use it in your classroom right away to help your learners develop and grow their reading skills.

Case in point: After Julia, the kindergarten teacher from Seattle, took my training and implemented the science of reading in her classroom, she reported, "I am so much more confident, and my kids are reading! It's not just that I feel good, it's that they feel good about who they are becoming as readers in my classroom."

Julia and her students are thriving because she finally has the keys she needs to unlock reading growth for *every* student in her class. She follows the step-by-step roadmap for teaching phonics skills, she uses five simple questions to help her students make letter–sound connections, and she has playful ways to teach phonological and phonemic awareness.

I want that same teaching confidence and student reading growth for you, and I'll be giving you all the strategies and tools you need to get them. Let's get this science of reading party started.

Chapter Two: How Brains *Really* Learn to Read

Spoiler Alert:
Instagram doesn't always get it right!

If you spend much time on social media, you've probably heard at least some of the many myths floating around about how students learn to read. Teachers often reach out to me to fact-check. Let's dispel three of the most common myths right away so we can begin grounding ourselves in research-backed truth.

Myth #1: Students *naturally* learn to read.

If you were taught the balanced-literacy approach as I was, or if you started teaching when whole language was popular, then you are likely familiar with this first reading myth. (It's the one I hear most often from teachers.)

For decades, educators believed students learned to read naturally just like they learned how to speak. The theory is that as long as we read aloud to them to model fluent reading and give them time to practice reading on their own, students can connect the dots, sound out words without much teacher guidance or intervention, and magically learn to read. As one of my education professors who taught this approach explained, "just get good books in kids' hands. They will figure out the rest!"

The Science of Reading in Action

Research has proven that is simply not true.

Nancy Young, a dyslexia expert, created an image called the Ladder of Reading to help illustrate what actually happens in an average class:

- 5 percent of students will learn to read with little intervention from a teacher.

- 35 percent of children will need some broad instruction so they can start making connections.

- 60 percent of the class (the vast majority) will require significant, direct lessons to help them make the connections they need to learn to read.

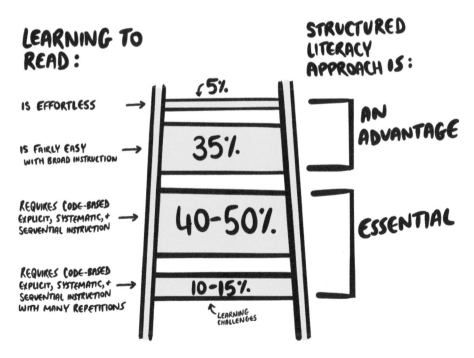

The Science of Reading in Action

Those stats are not surprising if we think about our evolutionary roots. Picture cave dwellers communicating 100,000 years ago when we first developed our anatomy for vocal tracts. Their grunts were a much simpler version of the complex language we use today. Although the groundwork for spoken language was still being imprinted in their early human brains, those neural pathways have now been evolving and strengthening for 100,000 years.

When we compare that evolution time to the meager 15,000 years we have been communicating through written language and the modest 5,000 years we have been using alphabetic systems, it is no wonder that most students need help learning how to read. Our brains have simply not had enough time to adapt and change.

Most babies come pre-wired to naturally learn spoken language and can figure out how to understand and communicate verbally simply by listening to the people around them, but babies do not arrive with all the neural pathways and brain capabilities they need to learn how to read. Instead, significant brain changes take place during the learning process.

In her book *Proust and the Squid*, Maryanne Wolf explains, "We were never born to read. No specific genes ever dictated reading's development. Human beings invented reading only a few thousand years ago. And with this invention, we rearranged the very organization of our brain, which in turn expanded the ways we were able to think, which altered the intellectual evolution of our species."

It is fascinating to realize that brains use their natural power for learning spoken language to establish these new reading abilities. For instance, brain scans show that an area in our visual cortex called the letter box is initially responsible for facial recognition. When students begin learning to recognize the unique shapes of letters, that area changes its role. The letter box becomes hyper-focused on *letter* recognition, and students' ability to remember faces moves from the left to the right hemisphere of their brain. It is as if a crane picks up the facial recognition function and drops it in another spot to make room for alphabetic letters.

Anatomically, our brains also build the new neural pathways we need to connect letters to their sounds. These fibers grow in number and strength as we practice reading. Just like a smooth superhighway enables cars to drive more quickly than a windy dirt road, our brains become able to retrieve sounds faster as the fibers are reinforced. With those new neural pathways, students' reading fluency increases.

As I mentioned earlier, studies show that only 5 percent of students can teach themselves how to read without support. The vast majority of students require specific instruction that builds those neural pathways and teaches them the skills they need to read. Professor Kerry Hempenstall explains, "explicit or direct instruction is the most effective teaching method, especially for the fundamental code-based components—phonemic awareness and phonics—and especially for children at-risk of reading failure."

It's time to officially put this falsehood to bed once and for all.

Myth Busted: Most children do not "naturally" learn to read. They must be taught how to read.

Myth #2: Guessing unknown words is an effective reading strategy.

Early in my career, I spent a day observing a veteran kindergarten teacher to gather ideas I could take back to my classroom. This teacher (let's call her Mrs. Poppins) had earned a well-respected reputation by staying current on educational trends and sprinkling her lessons with playful activities that kept her students engaged and on task. She was the teacher every parent wanted their child to have and every teacher wanted to become.

On this particular day, Mrs. Poppins led a reading strategy mini-lesson to show her kindergarteners what to do when they came to a word they did not know. On the pages of an oversized book, she had covered several of the largest words with Post-it® strips. With the class sitting attentively on the reading rug in front of her, Mrs. Poppins carefully pointed to each word as she read the story aloud. Every time she arrived at one of the words she had covered, she paused to build suspense. Then she set the stage and walked students through several problem-solving questions: "How exciting! We've come to another word we don't know. What could it be? *Hmmm*, let's put on our problem-solving caps and take a good guess. What word would make sense right now? Remember to look at the picture for clues!"

She gave the students a minute or so to think about the story, analyze the illustration on the page, and then turn to their neighbor to share a possible guess. Hearing their guesses, Mrs. Poppins focused students' attention on the *size* of the Post-it she had carefully cut to match the length of the word. "Would your guess look right in this space? Talk with your neighbor about

20

whether it is too long, too short, or just right. Remember, great readers are great detectives."

After giving the class time to adjust their predictions, Mrs. Poppins moved the Post-it slightly to display the first letter before asking students to problem solve again. "*Oooohhh…* The word starts with M. What sound does that letter say? Did your guess start with the /m/ sound? If not, turn to your neighbor and share a *new* guess. We want to make sure our prediction sounds right too."

With their final guesses locked in, Mrs. Poppins dramatically peeled off the Post-it to unveil the mystery word. The class sighed in unison—almost none of them had guessed correctly—but Mrs. Poppins quickly reinforced the three important questions students need to ask when they come to a word they do not know: 1. Does it make sense? 2. Does it sound right? 3. Does it look right?

Within five minutes, I was hooked. I decided right there that Mrs. Poppins was a genius. Teaching students to make educated guesses about unknown words and then use problem-solving skills to narrow in on the *actual* word was simply brilliant.

What I didn't know was that I was wrong.

The strategy Mrs. Poppins was using was called the three-cueing system. For decades, it was the backbone of popular programs, including Reading Recovery, Fountas and Pinnell, and Lucy Calkins' Units of Study. In 2019, an EdWeek Research Center survey found that 75 percent of kindergarten through second-grade teachers used the method to teach students how to read, and 65 percent of college of education professors taught it.

And yet, "since the 1960s, classroom studies of reading methods have consistently shown better results for early phonics instruction compared with instruction emphasizing meaning at the level of words and sentences. This effect is particularly strong for children at risk for reading failure."

Put simply, asking students to guess a word is *not* a reading strategy. It is a game. In fact, Ken Goodman, one of the creators of the three-cueing system, famously called it just that when he published an article titled "Reading: A Psycholinguistic Guessing Game."

Research from around the world continues to show that teaching students the skills they need to sound out words (rather than to guess words) creates far improved reading success. Australia's 2005 report *Teaching of Literacy* explains, "The incontrovertible finding from the extensive body of local and international evidence-based literacy research is that for children during the early years of schooling (and subsequently if needed) to be able to link their knowledge of spoken language to their knowledge of written language, they must first master the alphabetic code—the system of grapheme–phoneme correspondences that link written words to their pronunciations. Because these are both foundational and essential skills for the development of competence in reading, writing, and spelling, they must be taught explicitly, systematically, early, and well."

Likewise, the United Kingdom's 2006 report *Teaching of Early Reading* found "it is generally accepted that it is harder to learn to read and write in English because the relationship between sounds and letters is more complex than in many other alphabetic languages. It is therefore crucial to teach phonic work systematically, regularly and explicitly because children are highly unlikely to work out this relationship for themselves. It cannot be left to chance, or for children to ferret out, on their own, how the alphabetic code works."

In short, we can pull out our scissors and cut through another teaching myth because the research is clear: Helping students become fluent readers requires teaching them letter–sound connections, not problem-solving skills.

Myth busted: Guessing unknown words is not an effective reading strategy. Learning to sound out words is.

Myth #3: Reading is a completely visual task.

The third most common misconception I have seen is one that I believed for years too. It's the reason I had students cut apart two sets of sight word flashcards each week: one they could drill through at school and a second set they could bring home to recite after hours.

Because you are using your eyes to follow along with this text, it is natural to assume that the rest of the steps your brain is completing are also connected to sight. But that's simply not true! Yes, you do use your eyes to look at words, but that is where your visual work stops. Thanks to advances in neuroscience and technology, experts have tracked the brain areas and neural pathways that activate when we read, and it's clear that much of the work is not related to vision.

After your eyes scan the page to pull out letter chunks, syllables, prefixes, suffixes, and word roots, your brain instantly connects those clusters to the sounds they make. Then your brain pronounces those sounds in your head, and finally, you connect the sounds to their meaning.

HOW OUR BRAINS READ

1	2	3	4
SEE THE CLUSTER OF LETTERS	CONNECT THE CLUSTERS TO THE SOUNDS THEY MAKE	PRONOUNCE THE CLUSTERS IN YOUR HEAD	CONNECT IT TO THE MEANING
SHIP	SH = /sh/ I = /i/ P = /p/	/sh/ /ip/	

The Science of Reading in Action

If you are a young reader and see the letters SHIP on a page, your brain immediately changes them to the three sounds /sh/ /i/ /p/. That's steps one and two of the reading process. In step three, your brain blends those separate sounds to pronounce the word ship in your head like a record player and finally, in step four, you connect that word to its meaning and picture a *ship* sailing across the ocean.

As our ship example illustrates, step one is visual, but the rest of the process is not. After seeing the letter chunks, your brain instantly translates them into sounds that are blended together to make a word. In his book *Reading in the Brain*, Stanislas Dehaene explains, "proficient readers continue to use the sounds of words, even if they are unaware of it. . . . We do not have to move our lips, or even prepare an intention to do so. . . . We automatically access speech sounds while we read."

Fluent readers typically do not notice all of these steps because they happen so quickly. If we slow the process to a snail's pace, it becomes clear that only the first step of the reading involves eyesight.

Let's work through one more example before moving on to make sure these four steps of reading really click. If your eyes see the letters BAT, your brain immediately changes those letters to their sounds /b/, /a/, and /t/. Then it pronounces the sounds in your head as *bat*, before connecting that word to its meaning. Depending on what is happening in the story, your brain might picture a baseball bat, the nocturnal animal bat, or an athlete getting ready to hit a ball.

The Science of Reading in Action

The word *bat* (and every other word you have memorized through the years) is stored in an area of your brain called your orthographic lexicon. Imagine it as a library of file folders. Each folder contains a word's pronunciation, the letters used to make those sounds, and the various meanings of the word. The word folders are stored based on the letters used in the spelling, *not* pictures of what they look like. Here's why:

If humans stored words in a visual memory bank filled with pictures, our brains would need to be much larger. Every word folder would hold *thousands* of snapshots of various font types and sizes so that we could instantly recognize all the possible ways each word might look. If you memorized a word written in lowercase lettering, the moment you saw it in its uppercase form, you would have to learn that word again. Later, when you came across the word in cursive, you would need to memorize it once more. The process of reading would be tiresome and daunting for everyone—independent of their experience and skill.

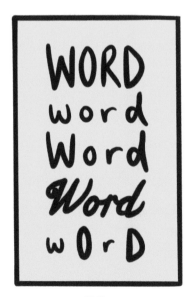

The Science of Reading in Action

Professor and researcher David Kilpatrick explains, "Because reading involves visual *input*, everyone presumed that it also involved visual *storage*. However, input and storage are not the same thing. . . . We do not store and retrieve words based on visual memory. Any strictly visually based teaching techniques represent an inefficient use of instructional time."

Teacher translation: We can throw away those sight word flashcards once and for all because students do not learn by visual drilling.

I love listening to audiobooks but I used to doubt whether they counted toward my reading goals since I was listening to a story instead of looking at one. When friends asked what I was reading, I always left out my Audible titles because I felt ashamed that I had not read the words with my eyes.

But research has proven that those audio stories absolutely count, and the benefits of reading them are extensive. Readers are exposed to a variety of dialects and are introduced to new vocabulary they can later add to their lexicon. Audio books build students' critical listening abilities and grow the love of reading for entertainment.

In reality, you are essentially acting as your own audiobook narrator every time you read anyway. Scans show that fluent readers use a network of brain regions at the same time. Most of these areas live in the language-processing area of the brain's left hemisphere—the same regions responsible for verbal communication:

- The *occipital-temporal region* manages letter and word recognition.

- The *parietal-temporal region* is responsible for sound–symbol connections and word analysis.

- The *frontal region* processes speech sounds.

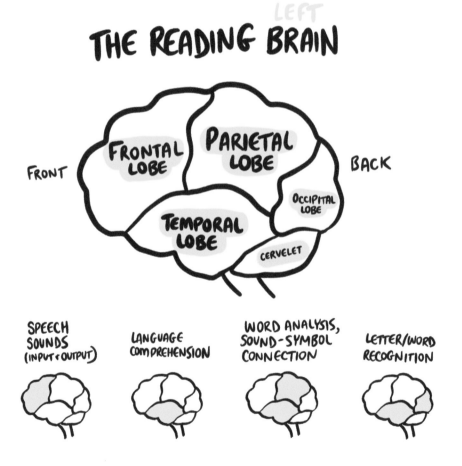

THE READING BRAIN

While each of these regions oversees a specific skill, they work together in almost constant collaboration. And that, my friend, means we can finally put this long-held myth to bed too.

Myth busted: Most of the reading process is not visual.

The Truth about How Brains Learn to Read

All of this myth-busting brings us to a million-dollar question: If so many long-held teaching theories are false, how do brains *really* learn to read?

Two popular science-based formulas answer this question. They are the basis for everything we will talk about going forward, so it is important that we take the time now to understand them.

Formula #1: The Simple View of Reading

First, let's look at the Simple View of Reading. Researchers Philip Gough and William Tunmer introduced this formula in 1986 during the height of the reading wars. It was designed to highlight the important role decoding skills play in students' reading comprehension and is essentially a math formula: a child's word reading multiplied by language comprehension equals reading comprehension.

What does each of those parts mean? Picture them as three different buckets that each hold a pile of specific skills.

THE HIGH LEVEL VIEW OF READING

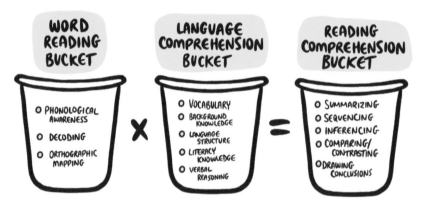

Word reading is a child's ability to see a word on a page and then sound it out. This bucket includes three key skills:

1. **Phonological awareness** is the ability to recognize and manipulate sounds in spoken language.

What sounds do you hear in the word cat? (Answer: /c/ /a/ /t/)

2. **Decoding** is translating written letters into the sounds they make.

What do the letters C-A-T spell? (Answer: Cat.)

3. **Orthographic mapping** means permanently connecting word spellings to their pronunciations and meaning.

Please read this word: CAT. (If the student reads the word immediately, it has been orthographically mapped.)

The Science of Reading in Action

Just like the name suggests, the word *reading* bucket contains the skills that empower students to sound out words. Children's decoding ability allows them to connect letters and letter clusters to the sounds they make. Phonological awareness enables them to blend those sounds to pronounce a complete word, and their orthographic mapping helps them remember that word the next time they see it by creating an easy-to-access file folder in their orthographic lexicon containing the spelling, pronunciation, and meaning.

Language comprehension is the second bucket in the Simple View of Reading. It describes a child's ability to understand and communicate with spoken language. The most important word in that definition is *spoken*. This bucket does not refer to a child's ability to comprehend what they are reading. Reading comprehension comes later.

Although children typically begin learning to talk around the age of one, they usually don't begin reading until they are at least four years old. Even then, at the earliest stages of reading, children's brains are focused more on sounding out words than thinking about what those words mean. Just like you could not simultaneously play a chess game, ride a bicycle, and cook dinner, new readers' brains are working so hard to connect letters to sounds that there is little room left to process what they're reading.

The good news is that, rather than waiting to build children's comprehension skills until their reading is more fluent, we can draw on students' much stronger verbal communication skills and develop them through speech.

The Science of Reading in Action

This *language comprehension* piece of the puzzle includes five different components:

1. **Vocabulary** is the ability to understand what words mean.

What is a BEE? (Answer: An insect that flies around collecting pollen and nectar to make honey.)

2. **Background knowledge** refers to the student's understanding of the concepts they are reading about.

We are going to read a book about bees. What do you know about them? (Answer: Sometimes bees sting people. I was stung by a bee once. Bees also make honey, and I eat that honey on my English muffins.)

3. *Language structure* is knowing the rules for building words and sentences. This skill set also includes readers' ability to recognize subtle differences between similar meanings.

If the prefix IL- means "not", what does the word illegal mean? (Answer: Not legal.)

4. **Literacy knowledge** refers to a reader's print concepts, including understanding the difference between letters and words and reading left to right across each page. It also includes knowing about types of text, including the difference between nonfiction and fiction.

Please put your fingers around a letter. Now put your fingers around a word. (Answer: The child might use their fingers to bracket the letter P and then use their fingers to frame the word PAL.)

5. And finally, **verbal reasoning** is the ability to think deeply about and make conclusions beyond what is actually said in the text.

Why do you think the stepmother was so mean to Cinderella? (Answer: I think she is not good at sharing. She wanted her daughters to have all of the clothes, food, and attention and did not want Cinderella to take any of that away from them.)

Language comprehension includes the skills students build as you ask them questions before, during, and after read-aloud stories. Although the word reading bucket covers *how* students read, language comprehension is *what* and *why* they read. It is everything that makes reading meaningful.

Up to this point, we have been focused on the left side of the equation and have studied the skills that go into reading. Now we are going to shift our focus to the right and look at the outcome.

The Simple View of Reading shows that when students can successfully read words and think deeply about what is being communicated, they have reading comprehension—the ability to understand and analyze what they are reading. This is where the magic happens! Students are able to sound out words on a page and, at the same time, understand what those written words mean. They are firing on all cylinders.

Similar to language comprehension discussed earlier, this

bucket also includes five skills:

1. **Summarizing** is the ability to highlight the most important events.

What are the most important things that happened in this story? (Answer: George fell and hit his head. He cried and his friend took him to the nurse. The nurse gave him a bandage and George felt better.)

2. **Sequencing** means retelling key parts of a story in the same order they occurred.

What happened in the beginning, middle, and end of this story? (Answer: First, the kids rode on the bus to go to the zoo. Then, they saw all of the animals and ate lunch. Finally, they went back to school so they could go home.)

3. **Inferencing** is reading between the lines and making guesses based on available information.

Why do you think the Big Bad Wolf wanted the pigs to open their doors? (Answer: He was hungry. I think he was having a hard time finding food. He could smell the pigs inside their house and was trying to trick them into opening their doors so that he could eat. I kind of feel bad for him. When I am really hungry like that, my stomach hurts.)

4. **Comparing and contrasting** means finding similarities and differences.

The Science of Reading in Action

We read ten different versions of Cinderella. What is the same about all of them? (Answer: Cinderella is always the main character, and she ends up finding her prince in the end.)

5. And finally, **drawing conclusions** is picking up on little hints and clues to read between the lines.

The author said the sun was coming up over the mountains. What time of day do you think it was? (Answer: It must have been morning because the sun rises at the beginning of the day.)

When students can read fluently enough that their brain can simultaneously think about what is happening, they have reading comprehension—the superpower that permits them to be entertained by stories and informed by nonfiction.

At first glance, the *Simple View of Reading* might appear to be pretty straightforward and uncomplicated, but its implications for early literacy are far-reaching. Why? It's all in the numbers.

Let's pretend that you sit down with one of your students to have her read a book about solar energy. That child's mother just happens to be a solar physicist, and family dinners are often filled with scientific discussions. Her language comprehension around this topic is out of this world—pun intended—and she can tell you everything you could ever wonder about solar panels and how they convert solar energy into electricity.

But there is a catch! The student is a brand-new reader, and the book you selected is filled with long, complicated words that are far beyond her word-reading abilities. It does not matter how much background knowledge she has on solar panels or how many scientific vocabulary words she knows—if she cannot read the words on the page, she cannot understand the book on her own. A zero in the word reading bucket means that her reading comprehension is going to be a zero, too, because our math formula shows $0 \times 1 = 0$.

THE HIGH LEVEL VIEW OF READING

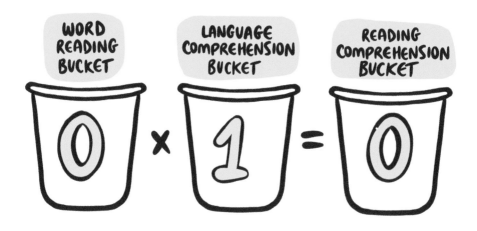

Now let's turn the tables and imagine that you sit down with a different child whose word-reading skills are so advanced that he can fluently read through a long list of whimsical wizard vocabulary in *Harry Potter*. But there is a different catch! This student is a new English Language Learner and does not understand even basic words that he is reading, let alone the book's magical potions and fanciful vocabulary. The child might be able to sound out the words quickly, but he will have no picture playing in his brain as he reads the story. As this example illustrates, even with the most amazing word-reading ability, if students have zero language comprehension, they also have zero reading comprehension because $1 \times 0 = 0$.

THE HIGH LEVEL VIEW OF READING

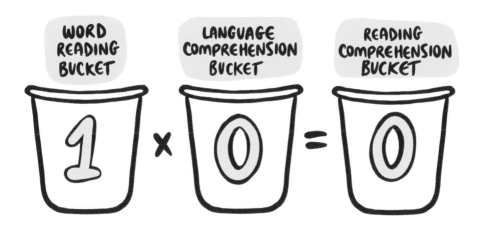

Although weakness in word reading is often identified early in children's reading development because you can hear students struggling to sound out, holes in language comprehension may not present themselves until later. Why? When students are first learning to read, their practice texts are typically filled with simple, short words, such as *cat, run*, and *mom*. It's not until readers are exposed to text with more complicated vocabulary words and concepts that their weakness in language comprehension is exposed.

We will talk about teaching strategies you can use to shore up any weaknesses in this area later. For now, just remember that word reading and language comprehension are both critical pieces of the puzzle, and the Simple View of Reading formula is helpful for understanding successful reading growth.

Formula #2: The Reading Rope

Before we move on, let's look at one more popular science of reading formula called *Scarborough's Reading Rope* so that we can solidify our understanding of how students learn to read at a 30,000-foot view. Designed by researcher Hollis Scarborough, the concept aligns closely with the *Simple View of Reading*. The difference is in the packaging. The infographic illustrates how students' language-comprehension and word-recognition skills work collaboratively to build reading comprehension and fluency.

To understand the *Reading Rope*, imagine that each of the language-comprehension and word-recognition skills is an individual piece of thread. As students develop their abilities through explicit teaching and practice, those skills become more automatic and begin working together with increased efficiency. Like the players on a team who know each other's strengths and weaknesses, areas of the brain become better adept at collaborating. The threads of skills twist tighter and tighter, making it difficult to identify any specific one because they are all interconnected. As a result of the increasingly strategic teamwork and automaticity of the skills, students' fluency and comprehension strengthen, and children become progressively proficient at reading.

Our goal is to move students from the left side of the *Reading Rope* to the right, and that's exactly what we're jumping into next. But before we do, let's check off a few important action steps.

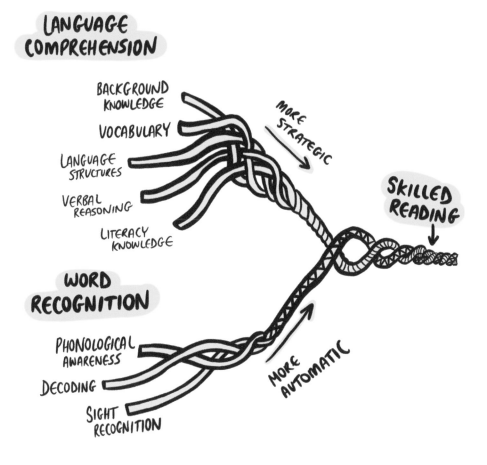

Call to Action

Research has proven that deliberate practice is key to evolving from novice to expert, so I'll be giving you simple follow-up activities at the end of every chapter to make it easier for you to learn concepts and implement new strategies.

Don't skip these sections! They provide the fast track you need to grow your teaching confidence and help all your students get bigger reading growth. To use an adage, practice really will make perfect.

1. Scan the QR code to the right and print out the tricky terms sheet. Then slide it into your reading binder for easy access so you never have to spend time looking up those terms again.

SCAN ME

2. Hop over to your favorite social media site and share one reason you're excited to dive into the science of reading along with the hashtag #scienceofreadinginaction.

(You can connect with other like-minded teachers who are using that hashtag too!) The team and I are eager to cheer you on.

Chapter Three: Phonological Awareness Isn't Just for Kindergarteners

The first time I heard about phonological awareness, my hands started to sweat. I didn't know what the phrase meant, but something deep in my gut told me those two words were about to turn my world upside down. Boy, was that an understatement!

To understand what the term means, it helps to focus on the very first syllable: *phon*. That root comes from the Greek word *phonos* which means *sound* or *voice*. Just like you hear your friend talking on a telephone, phonological awareness means hearing the sounds in spoken language and being able to successfully move and change them. Because the skill is focused entirely on sound, you can do it with your eyes closed.

For decades, research has identified phonological awareness as a critical key to unlocking students' reading growth. (You will remember that it holds the first spot in our Simple View of Reading's word reading bucket.) Phonological awareness is often referred to as an "umbrella term" because it includes five different types of skills:

- **Word awareness**
- **Syllable awareness**
- **Rhyming awareness**
- **First sound awareness**
- **Phonemic awareness**

The Science of Reading in Action

In the earliest stages of phonological awareness, children focus on large units of sound, including whole words. The more they practice and learn, their brains become able to identify and manipulate increasingly smaller units of sound. This word awareness eventually enables students to recognize syllables, then rhymes, beginning sounds, and finally, phonemic awareness —the ability to hear and manipulate individual sounds in words called *phonemes*. Phonemic awareness skills make up the most advanced phase of phonological awareness because they require children to successfully home in on single phonemes.

Let's picture how the learning process might play out in your class during a simple writing activity. Imagine asking your students to write the sentence "The sun is yellow." As you speak, your brand new readers will be able to identify the four words you say: the, sun, is, yellow. However, they will be hard-pressed to link any of those whole words to the letters used to spell them. (Is there a letter that spells sun?)

Meanwhile, students who have developed phonemic awareness will hear you say that same sentence, but after they identify the whole words, they will parse out the individual sounds. They will stretch the word sun into the three distinct phonemes /s/ /u/ /n/ and will break the word is into just two: /i/ /z/.

Recognizing those phonemes gives this second group of students a noticeable advantage when it comes to spelling because they can hear the sounds they are being asked to connect to written letters. It is not surprising, then, that phonemic awareness has been named the best predictor of early reading success. When the National Reading Panel published its 2000 report, it identified more than fifty "gold standard" studies verifying phonemic awareness as a critical component of effective reading and spelling instruction. Long-term data has shown the depth of this skill is a better predictor of later reading achievement than IQ tests or verbal reasoning abilities. David Kilpatrick explains, "Every point in a child's development of word-level reading is substantially affected by phonological awareness, from learning letter names all the way up to efficiently adding new, multi-syllabic words to the sight vocabulary."

THE HIGH LEVEL VIEW OF READING

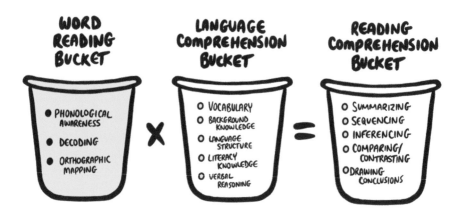

WORD READING BUCKET
- PHONOLOGICAL AWARENESS
- DECODING
- ORTHOGRAPHIC MAPPING

X

LANGUAGE COMPREHENSION BUCKET
- VOCABULARY
- BACKGROUND KNOWLEDGE
- LANGUAGE STRUCTURE
- LITERACY KNOWLEDGE
- VERBAL REASONING

=

READING COMPREHENSION BUCKET
- SUMMARIZING
- SEQUENCING
- INFERENCING
- COMPARING/ CONTRASTING
- DRAWING CONCLUSIONS

Students' ability to hear and manipulate the sounds in words is such an essential piece of the puzzle that many literacy experts recommend practicing it every day from preschool through second grade so that children receive the training their brains need to master it. Just like a house cannot be steady and strong if the foundation has cracks, readers are likely to struggle if they have gaps in their phonological awareness skills. That is why, when upper elementary or middle school teachers reach out to me for help with a struggling reader in their class, the first question I always ask is whether they have assessed the child's phonemic awareness to detect any holes. Because weak phonemic awareness is the most common factor in struggling readers' difficulties, analyzing it is absolutely crucial. The great news is that it is never too late to provide the training to students—or even adults—who still need to master this skill.

Early in the spring of 2022, a fourth-grade teacher named Kim joined my Reading Roadmap training searching for answers. In the past, most of her students began the year reading fluently, so she was able to focus her time and attention on reading to learn rather than learning to read. But after the pandemic, things had changed—*dramatically*. When students returned to school that year, her roster included a dozen struggling readers who labored to sound out words, and Kim was desperate to help them.

The first week into the challenge, Kim learned about phonological awareness and decided to test several students to see whether they had any holes. And they did! She began practicing phonological awareness every day and within weeks she saw noticeable results. Students who had been stuck began making progress. One afternoon, a student looked up at her with a huge smile and said, "Wow! I can read sentences, not just words."

Clearly, phonological awareness is not just for kindergarteners anymore.

Before we dive into the simple but effective ways you can help your students master these skills, let's take a 30,000-foot view of each phase of phonological awareness.

Spoiler Alert:

These skills are presented in order from least to most difficult so you can picture how they build on one another. However, researcher Dr. Susan Brady, a professor at the University of Rhode Island, emphasizes that they do *not* need to be taught in order. In fact, the skills that are most closely tied to students' reading success are at the phoneme level we will discuss at the end. "We can really improve what's happening by zeroing in on *phoneme* awareness right at the beginning of kindergarten, and importantly, connecting it with letter knowledge right away."

Type One: Word Awareness

Although you may not have noticed it before, spoken language is essentially a long string of sounds. To process it, our brain needs to divide those sounds into meaningful units called words. If you have ever turned off the subtitles when you were listening to a movie in an unfamiliar language, you know how challenging it is to separate conversations into meaningful units when you are unable to even identify the start and finish of each word. That is the same challenge students face in the earliest stage of phonological awareness.

Luckily, helping children learn to identify individual words can be as simple as practicing sentence segmenting. Just as the name suggests, sentence segmenting means breaking a sentence into individual parts by counting the number of words they hear. Let's work through a couple of different sentence segmenting examples so you can see how to stretch the activity and make it increasingly more difficult as students learn.

Start by having students count the words in short and simple two- and three-word sentences:

- "Stop that." (Answer: Two words.)
- "Let go." (Answer: Two words.)
- "They went home." (Answer: Three words.)
- "This is yummy." (Answer: Three words.)

When students have mastered basic sentence segmenting and are ready for a greater challenge, increase the number of words in the sentences:

- "The bird is flying." (Answer: Four words.)
- "I ate my lunch." (Answer: Four words.)
- "We went to the store." (Answer: Five words.)
- "He gave me his toy." (Answer: Five words.)

SENTENCE SEGMENTING

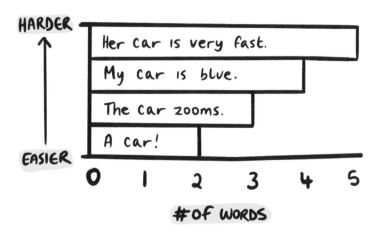

Remember, this is not a race! Go slow to go fast. For many children, it will take time and daily practice to form the neural pathways their brains need to be successful with longer sentences. Similar to increasing your dumbbell weights slowly over time so you can boost your arm strength, the goal is to help students progressively develop their brain muscles too.

Type Two: Syllable Awareness

Once students can divide sentences into individual words, they have the necessary foundation for the next phase of phonological awareness: syllable awareness. In this phase, instead of breaking *sentences* into words, children will break *words* into syllables—units of spoken language that have one vowel sound each. For instance, the word elephant breaks into three syllables: el - e - phant. Or they could break apart the word elbow into both of its syllables: el - bow.

Notice that those examples (like every English word) have only one vowel sound in each syllable. Because vowels are made with an open, unobstructed mouth, children can feel syllables by placing a hand under their chins when they say a word. Each time the student feels their chin tap their hand, they are hearing a new syllable. Try it with your name! Each chin tap is a separate syllable.

Although English has only six vowel letters—*A, E, I, O, U*, and sometimes *Y*—there are fifteen different vowel *sounds*. That total jumps to eighteen when you add the r-controlled vowel sounds /er/ /ar/ and /or/. Vowel sounds are the peak of each syllable and the thing we sing. You can give this fact a test run by trying to sing "Happy Birthday" without any vowels and then sing it again the normal way. It is amazing how much easier vowels make it.

When children are learning to use vowel sounds to break words into syllables, it is helpful to practice an activity called syllable tapping. Based on the Total Physical Response or TPR teaching method, syllable tapping creates a brain link between a speech output and an action that results in improved language learning. To do it, touch the top of your hand as you say the first syllable in a word. Then, as you say the second syllable, pat your elbow. Tap your shoulder with the third syllable and the top of your head for the fourth.

Taking a moment to practice syllable tapping now will help make it stick, so let's work through a few examples. Tap out:

Scan the QR code to see it in action.

SCAN ME

- Cat (Answer: "Cat" with one tap on top of your hand.)
- Birthday (Answer: "Birth" tap your hand. "Day" tap your elbow.)
- Alligator (Answer: "Al" tap your hand. "Li" tap your elbow. "Ga" tap your shoulder. "Tor" tap your head.)
- Rainbow (Answer: "Rain" tap your hand. "Bow" tap your elbow.)

Syllable tapping is a fantastic way to build students' phonological awareness. It's also a handy little time filler to pull out during those random three-minute chunks that pop up throughout your school day. You can use whisper voices and tap in the hallway waiting for lunch or tap as a brain break before you transition to math. The opportunities for practice are endless, as are the words you use! For example, students love tapping classmates' names. You can also make the activity themed by using seasonal words such as *pumpkin* and *scarecrow*.

Syllable tapping is one of those activities that never seems to get old, but, similar to sentence segmenting, it is important to be patient and grow students' syllable awareness over time so their brains have the chance to establish the capacity and neural pathways they need to be successful. Start with one- and two-syllable words and then, when children master those, stretch their skills by moving on to words with more syllables. Eventually, your learners will be able to break apart words like *dictionary*, *calculator,* and *avocado*.

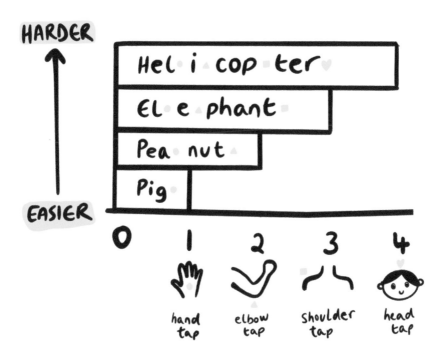

Type Three: Rhyme Awareness

I am willing to bet that you are already familiar with this next phase of phonological awareness because rhyming is a common part of many poems, songs, and books. The technical definition of rhyming is *two or more words ending in the same sound*. But what you may not realize is that the ending sound has a name: *rime* (same pronunciation, different spelling and meaning).

A syllable's rime starts with the vowel sound and continues through any consonants that follow it. For instance, the syllable *in* starts with the vowel sound /i/ and continues through the /n/ that comes afterward. The syllable *op* starts with the vowel sound /o/ and continues through the /p/.

Sounds in a syllable that come before a rime begins are called the *onset.* So a syllable like cat has the onset /c/ and the rime /at/. Not every syllable has an onset, but every syllable does have a rime, so when you are analyzing syllables, it is helpful to find the vowel sound first. Then you know that anything before that vowel is the onset, and anything after the onset is part of the rime.

Let's work through a few quick examples. Name the onset and rime in these words:

- Fin (Answer: /F/ is the onset and /in/ is the rime.)
- Dish (Answer: /D/ is the onset and /ish/ is the rime.)
- Then (Answer: /Th/ is the onset and /en/ is the rime.)
- Check (Answer: /Ch/ is the onset and /eck/ is the rime.)

And just for fun bonus points, name the onset and rime in these two challenge words:

- On (Answer: There is no onset but /on/ is the rime.)
- It (Answer: There is no onset but /it/ is the rime.)

Now that you conquered our quick onset and rime party, you also know that rhyming with a Y is focused on the ending rimes in words because rhyming words end in the same sounds. For instance, the rhyming pair *cat* and *bat* both end with the /at/ rime, and the rhyming pair *hog* and *log* end with the /og/ rime. A quick, fun way to help children strengthen their rhyming muscles is to say a pair of words aloud and have them show you two thumbs up if the words rhyme or a thumb down if they do not. Let's practice:

- Cat and bat. (Answer: Two thumbs up)
- Dog and fish. (Answer: One thumb down)
- Hop and ant. (Answer: One thumb down)
- Jelly and belly. (Answer: Two thumbs up)

It is a simple game, but kids love it!

Other fun options include reading rhyming books, singing nursery rhymes, and even brainstorming words that belong to a specific word family. ("Let's see how many words we can name in thirty seconds that end in /ug/!")

Type Four: First Sound Awareness

Moving right along, lucky number four on the phonological awareness list is first sound awareness, and it focuses on those onsets we were just identifying. First sound awareness means hearing the beginning sounds in words. This skill is also commonly associated with alliteration because it can be used to match two or more words that start with the same sound. "Taco Tuesday" might be one of the most famous examples, but there are plenty of others we could brainstorm, including tongue twisters like "Peter Piper picked a peck of pickled peppers" and even names: "Mickey Mouse."

Practicing alliteration is as simple as naming two different words and having students notice whether they start with the same sound. If they do, the children will clap twice. If they do not, they will clap just once.

Scan the QR code to see it in action.

- Box and beach. (Answer: Two claps)
- Foot and car. (Answer: One clap)
- Apple and attic. (Answer: Two claps)
- Chip and think. (Answer: One clap

SCAN ME

This activity focuses on *sounds* rather than spellings, so it is important to turn off your fluent reader brain and just listen to the words instead of thinking about the actual letters that are used to spell them. Why? Every so often you will come across a tricky pair of words. Knob and neck, for instance, start with different letters but have the same beginning sound. Awesome and octopus are a first sound pair too. If you were practicing alliteration, your fluent reader brain could easily ring unnecessary false alarms when, in fact, they *do* start with the same beginning sound. It helps to remember that phonological awareness can be done with your eyes closed; the focus is on sounds, not letters.

Type Five: Phoneme Awareness

Last but definitely not least is phonemic awareness—the ultimate of all phonological awareness skills. This phase has a profound impact on students' learning and future reading success. A phoneme is an individual sound. When you break apart the sounds in the word cat, for instance, you will hear three separate phonemes: /c/ /a/ /t/. If you pull apart the word jump, you will hear four: /j/ /u/ /m/ /p/.

To practice, name the phonemes in each of these words:

- Book (Answer: /b/ /oo/ /k/
- Rain (Answer: /r/ /ai/ /n/)
- Duck (Answer: /d/ /u/ /k/)
- Shop (Answer: /sh/ /o/ /p/)

The Science of Reading in Action

Notice that each of these examples has four letters but just three phonemes. Why is that possible? Many sounds are made with letter combinations. SH and CK are great examples of two letters that work together to make just one sound. The key to successful phoneme identification is listening for the sounds you hear instead of thinking about the spellings. Admittedly, that can be tricky for fluent readers at first, but with practice, it gets easier.

Because phonemes are individual sounds, phonemic awareness is the ability to hear those sounds and then move them around in different ways. As with the other phonological awareness skills, the skills are presented here from simplest to most complex.

If you are working with brand new readers who are not yet familiar with letters, practice these skills by simply saying the prompts and having them reply verbally. Once students have been introduced to letters, however, it is important to pair the verbal prompts with the letters used to spell them. (Having children write on lap-sized white boards is great for this!) The International Dyslexia Association's 2022 Phoneme Awareness Fact Sheet explains: "When teaching and practicing phoneme awareness skills, once the student has become aware of the phoneme, linking each speech sound with the grapheme that spells it will facilitate the transfer of skills to reading and writing."

Check out the Staircase of Phonemic Awareness Skill Difficulty graphic on the next page.

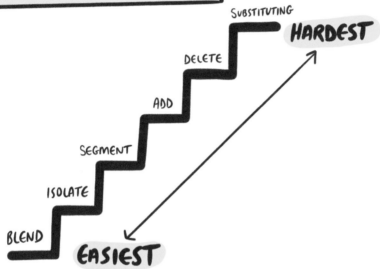

1. Blending phonemes
2. Isolating phonemes
3. Segmenting phonemes
4. Adding phonemes
5. Deleting phonemes
6. Substituting phonemes

The first phonemic awareness skill students' brains are ready to tackle is *blending phonemes*. As the name suggests, when children are practicing, they will blend individual sounds to make a word. To practice, string these sounds together and name the word:

- /p/ /e/ /n/ (Answer: Pen)
- /c/ /ow/ (Answer: Cow)
- /b/ /a/ /th/ (Answer: Bath)
- /g/ /oa/ /t/ (Answer: Goat)

SCAN ME

With practice, students will soon be ready to start working on the next level of difficulty: *isolating phonemes*. If someone is sick with a contagious disease, they isolate themselves to avoid spreading the illness to other people. That same concept applies here. When you are isolating phonemes, you pull out a specific sound, like this:

- What is the first sound you hear in the word *bun?* (Answer: /b/)
- What is the last sound you hear in the word *bun?* (Answer: /n/)
- What is the middle sound you hear in the word *bun?* (Answer: /u/)

SCAN ME

Notice that the order we practiced isolating phonemes was first sound, last sound, and *then* middle sound. It may seem like a small detail, but it is incredibly important developmentally. Students' brains are first able to identify beginning sounds. Soon, they also become able to hear ending sounds, but most children will need additional time to successfully hear and identify those middle vowels. When you are mapping phoneme isolation practice, remember the order: beginning, ending, middle. It's strange but true.

Elkonin Boxes are one of my favorite ways to help students begin isolating phonemes because they turn the abstract listening action into a concrete activity children can see and feel. The technique gets its name from the Russian psychologist D. B. El'konin, who developed it in the 1960s.

First, you will pronounce a word and have your student repeat it. For this example, let's use the word dog. After the child has repeated the word correctly, have them count the number of phonemes they hear and draw a box or square for each phoneme. In our example, dog has three sounds (/d/ /o/ /g/) so the student would draw three boxes, like this:

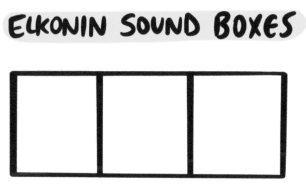

Next, you'll help the child understand that each sound is connected to something by having them slide one counting chip, Unifix cube, or other manipulative into a box as they say each phoneme.

/d/ (Slide a chip into the first box.)
/o/ (Slide a chip into the second box.)
/g/ (Slide a chip into the third box.)

To reinforce blending, ask the child to slide their finger underneath the boxes from left to right as they combine the phonemes to say *dog*.

When students are ready, you can make the practice more challenging by having them replace the manipulatives they slide into each Elkonin box with the letters used to spell the sounds. But starting with the hands-on activity first helps learners' brains build rock-solid phoneme isolation capabilities.

Speaking of stretching students, they will eventually be ready to segment phonemes. You have already segmented sentences and syllables, so you know that segmenting means to break apart. Segmenting phonemes, then, is separating the individual sounds in words:

- Name the sounds in frog.
  (Answer: /f/ /r/ /o/ /g/)
- Name the sounds in tin.
  (Answer: /t/ /i/ /n/)
- Name the sounds in bell.
  (Answer: /b/ /e/ /l/)

SCAN ME

60

Next up is adding phonemes. The most important thing to remember when you are practicing this skill is that you are adding *sounds,* not letters:

- Add /c/ to the beginning of *rest*. What is the new word? (Answer: *Crest*)
- Add /s/ to the end of *girl*. What is the new word? (Answer: *Girls*)
- Add /b/ to the beginning of *raid*. What is the new word? (Answer: *Braid*)

Eventually, students will be ready to work on deleting phonemes by taking away one of the sounds in a word, like this:

- Take away /b/ in *band*. What is the new word? (Answer: *And*)
- Take away /d/ in *walked*. What is the new word? (Answer: *Walk*)
- Take away /ch/ in *chat.* What is the new word? (Answer: *At*)

The most difficult phonemic awareness skill children will tackle is substituting phonemes—swapping one sound out for a new one.

- Change /m/ in *mat* to /h/. What is the new word? (Answer: Hat)
- Change /g/ in *go* to /n/. What is the new word? (Answer: No)
- Change /s/ in *sun* to /f/. What is the new word? (Answer: Fun)

With consistent, direct instruction and practice, your students' phonemic awareness skills will grow and strengthen as they become increasingly better at hearing and manipulating sounds in more complicated words. When they once labored to blend the sounds /h/ /u/ /g/ to say the word *hug*, with instruction and experience, children will eventually be able to quickly substitute the /r/ in *grow* for /l/ to make a new word *glow*. And *that* superpower will help them master the next critical batch of skills: phonics.

PHONOLOGICAL AWARENESS

WORD AWARENESS	SYLLABLE AWARENESS
DISTINGUISH SEPARATE WORDS IN A SENTENCE EX: "COUNT THE WORDS YOU HEAR: THE CAR IS BLUE" (ANSWER: 4)	SEPARATE WORDS INTO SYLLABLES EX: "BREAK 'ELEPHANT' INTO PARTS." (ANSWER: EL-E-PHANT)
RHYMING AWARENESS	**FIRST SOUND AWARENESS**
IDENTIFY AND PRODUCE WORDS THAT END WITH THE SAME SOUNDING FINAL SYLLABLE EX: "DO 'CAT' AND 'POP' RHYME?" (ANSWER: NO)	IDENTIFY AND PRODUCE WORDS THAT START WITH THE SAME SOUND EX: "BRAINSTORM WORDS THAT START WITH THE SAME SOUND AS 'CASSIE'!" (ANSWER: CAT, CARING, CALM...)

PHONEMIC AWARENESS	
HEARING AND MANIPULATING THE INDIVIDUAL SOUNDS IN WORDS	
PHONEME ISOLATION	**PHONEME BLENDING**
IDENTIFYING A SPECIFIC SOUND IN A WORD EX: "WHAT'S THE FIRST SOUND IN 'RED'?" (ANSWER: /R/)	STRINGING TOGETHER INDIVIDUAL SOUNDS TO MAKE A WORD EX: "BLEND THESE SOUNDS /P/ /I/ /o/ TOGETHER WHAT'S THE WORD?" (ANSWER: PIE)
PHONEME SEGMENTATION	**PHONEME ADDITION**
BREAKING THE INDIVIDUAL SOUNDS IN WORDS EX: "WHAT DO YOU HEAR IN 'JET'?" (ANSWER: /J/ /E/ /T/)	ADDING ANOTHER SOUND TO WORDS EX: "ADD /G/ TO THE BEGINNING OF 'OAT'. WHAT'S THE NEW WORD?" (ANSWER: GOAT)
PHONEME DELETION	**PHONEME SUBSTITUTION**
TAKING AWAY SOUNDS FROM WORDS EX: TAKE AWAY THE /R/ FROM 'CLOVER'. WHAT'S THE NEW WORD? (ANSWER: CLOVE)	SWAPPING ONE SOUND IN A WORD FOR ANOTHER EX: "CHANGE /P/ IN 'MAP' TO /T/. WHAT'S THE NEW WORD?" (ANSWER: MAT)

Bonus Fact

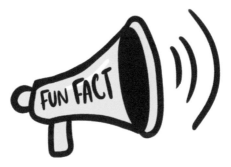

The Yale Center for Dyslexia and Creativity reports dyslexia is "very common, affecting 20 percent of the population and representing 80 to 90 percent of all those with learning disabilities." That means in your classroom right now, on average, one out of every five students is dyslexic.

Dyslexia is a neurobiological disorder associated with reading and spelling difficulty. Depending on the person, it can affect a variety of different skills, including working memory, letter knowledge, and the ability to rapidly name things, but the most commonly linked deficit is in phonological processing. Dyslexia can't be cured, but early intervention and consistent practice have been proven to dramatically improve students' reading success. The two key words are early intervention. In 2016, David Kilpatrick explained, "Early training of phonological awareness in kindergarten and first grade prevents many reading difficulties from happening in the first place."

That is incredibly empowering! As you are lesson planning, teaching, assessing, and practicing phonological awareness, you will be supporting all of your students, but especially children with dyslexia.

Call to Action

1. Add phonological awareness practice to your lesson plans right away by scanning the QR code and printing out two weeks of no-prep, ready-to-use daily warmups.

SCAN ME

2. Snap a photo of your favorite phonological awareness warmup and share it on social media to inspire other teachers to try it too!
#scienceofreadinginaction

MY NOTES

Chapter Four: The Phonics Rules Every Child Needs to Learn

For years, I called common words like *the* and *have* "rule breakers" and told my kindergarteners, "You just need to memorize them." Have similar words ever come out of your mouth?

Well, I was wrong—very, very wrong.

We can use thirty-one different phonics and spelling rules to explain between 96 and 98 percent of English words, including *the* and *have.* Although, like me, you may not have learned the rules when you were in school, once you know what they are, you will be amazed by how empowered you feel to demystify them for your students.

Unlike phonological awareness which is entirely auditory and could be done with your eyes closed, phonics involves connecting written letters on a page to the sounds they make. Unless you are reading braille, you will need to have your eyes open to practice.

Phonics is a little like code-breaking; letters and letter combinations can be linked to specific sounds, and when we know those sounds, we can figure out the code to read them. The letter *B*, for instance, makes the /b/ sound, and the letters *CH* create the /ch/ sound. Just like a detective can break secret picture codes by matching a symbol to the letter it represents, students break the reading code by connecting written letters to their sounds. With a solid understanding of letter–sound connections, children can blend the sounds and decode words—the second skill in the *Simple View of Reading's* word reading bucket.

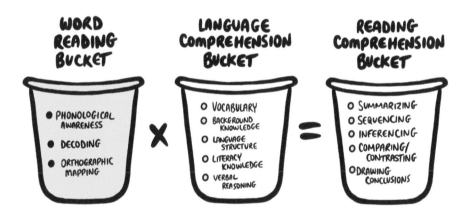

By now, we have debunked the long-held myth that children learn to read naturally and without help. Research has shown that most students learn best through guided, intentional, systematic lessons and practice. Teaching children phonics is the difference between asking them to solve an encrypted message without help and solving that same message with a code-breaking cipher. This cipher empowers children to turn a book filled with meaningless circles, lines, and shapes into one of spellbinding stories and enlightening discoveries.

The Science of Reading in Action

Although new readers need extra time and effort for their brains to translate letters on a page into the correct sounds, fluent readers can instantly decode words without conscious awareness. That automaticity is our ultimate teaching goal, but building it takes practice. Researcher Linnea Ehri's analysis of thirty-eight phonics studies explains, "Because the writing system in English is more complex and variable than in some languages, it is harder to learn, making systematic phonics instruction even more important to teach, because children will have difficulty figuring out the system on their own." This reality is why I always recommend working through two phases of phonics lessons: the plunge and the deep dive.

Phase One: The Plunge

For most new readers, written letters (also called graphemes) start as meaningless shapes on a piece of paper. The letter *G* is just as random and nonsensical to new readers as an arbitrary squiggle.

To help children understand that letters are actually secret written codes for sounds, you can teach them a helpful alphabet chant that connects each letter to its sound, a word it starts with, and a corresponding action like this:

"A is for apple. /ă/ /ă/ /ă/."

(Hold your hand to your mouth as if you are biting into an apple.)

B is for baby. /b/ /b/ /b/."
(Pretend to rub your eyes with your hands as if you are crying.)

"C is for cat. /c/ /c/ /c/."
(Draw imaginary whiskers on your face.)

Because the goal in this first phase is simple awareness of the letter–sound connection rather than actual memorization, you can teach the chant quickly. In my kindergarten class, I added five new letters each day so that we could practice the entire chant from *A* to *Z* in a little over a week. Although most of my kindergartners did not learn all of the letters and sounds in that short time, they began understanding that those once random shapes they saw in books, on walls, and on billboards were not as arbitrary as they once seemed.

The key to this activity is its multisensory approach. Children *see* an alphabet flashcard, *say* the chant, and *do* the action. This helps their brains quickly connect the written letter with the letter name and sound. Multisensory learning has proven benefits because it engages multiple areas of the brain at the same time. Not only are students developing neural pathways based on visual inputs but they are simultaneously building fibers based on auditory (sound), and kinesthetic (movement) inputs. It is a supercharging trifecta of brain growth!

The alphabet chant is a powerful tool for lightning-fast connection building, but repetition is critical. Add four of five new letters each morning and practice all of the letters you have learned several times throughout the day to help children reinforce their learning.

ALPHABET CHANT

The key to this activity is having the kids **see** the alphabet flashcard, **say** the chant and **do** the action at the same time to help their brains quickly connect the written letter with the letter name and sound. Introduce 4-5 new letters each morning and practice several times throughout the day.

What to Say	What to Do
A is for apple, /a/ /a/ /a/. And A is for alien, /ae/ /ae/ /ae/.	Hold your hand up to your mouth like you're eating an apple. Then place your pointer fingers on your forehead and point.
B is for baby, /b/ /b/ /b/.	Tuck your hands into fists and pretend to rub your eyes like a baby who's crying.
C is for cat, /c/ /c/ /c/.	Point with two fingers on both hands and wipe the sides of your cheeks to make whiskers.
D is for dog, /d/ /d/ /d/.	Crouch down like a sitting dog.
E is for elbow, /e/ /e/ /e/. And E is for ear, /ee/ /ee/ /ee/.	Point to your elbow several times. Then tug your ear.
F is for four, /f/ /f/ /f/.	Hold up four fingers.
G is for goat, /g/ /g/ /g/.	Make goat horns holding both pointer fingers on top of your head.
H is for house, /h/ /h/ /h/.	Place your hands together over your head to make a roof.
I is for iguana, /i/ /i/ /i/. And I is for icicle, /ie/ /ie/ /ie/.	Hold four fingers on top of your head to make an iguana crest. Then pull your hand down like your pulling an icicle.
J is for jump rope, /j/ /j/ /j/.	Hop up and down like you're jumping with a jump rope.
K is for kangaroo /k/ /k/ /k/.	Jump high like a kangaroo as you hold your bent hands to your chest to make short arms.
L is for lion, /l/ /l/ /l/.	Spread your fingers on both hands and touch one thumb to each cheek to make a lion mane.

SCAN ME

Scan the QR code to download my alphabet flashcards and see the chant in action.

70

The Science of Reading in Action

What to Say	What to Do
M is for monkey, /m/ /m/ /m/.	Bend your arms and pretend to scratch your armpits like a monkey.
N is for nose, /n/ /n/ /n/.	Point to your nose.
O is for octopus, /o/ /o/ /o/. And O is for ocean, /oe/ /oe/ /oe/.	Stretch out your arms and wave them in the air like octopus arms. Then move your arms like you are swimming in the ocean.
P is for pirate, /p/ /p/ /p/.	Place your hands together to make a pirate spyglass next to your eye.
Q is for queen, /q/ /q/ /q/.	Hold four fingers above your head to make a crown.
R is for robot, /r/ /r/ /r/.	Bend your arms in jerky, robot-like movements.
S is for soup, /s/ /s/ /s/.	Pretend to dip a spoon into a soup bowl and eat it.
T is for tornado, /t/ /t/ /t/.	Spin one finger in the air to make a swirling tornado.
U is for up, /u/ /u/ /u/. And U is for unicorn, /ue/ /ue/ /ue/.	Point up with your hands several times. Then place a hand at your forehead to form a unicorn horn.
V is for vacuum, /v/ /v/ /v/.	Pretend to vacuum with one arm.
W is for watch, /w/ /w/ /w/.	Tap your wrist with your pointer finger like you are pointing to a watch.
X is for mix, /x/ /x/ /x/.	Use your fist to stir an imaginary bowl of dough.
Y is for yo-yo, /y/ /y/ ./y/.	Pretend to yo-yo.
Z is for zipper, /z/ /z/ /z/.	Grab an imaginary zipper and pull it up and down your chest.

SCAN ME

Scan the QR Code to see a video of me doing the chant!

71

Phase Two: The Deep Dive

After introducing students to letter–sound connections, it is time to begin phase two and closely analyze each sound. This deep dive on each letter teaches children the phonogram and spelling rules they will use to eventually become fluent readers and spellers. *Phono* means *sound*, and *gram* means *written symbol*. When children are learning about the phonogram H, they will be connecting the /h/ sound to the written letter H. That pairing is the H phonogram.

In some languages, every sound has its own written symbol. That is not the case in English, however. The twenty-six alphabet letters are used to make twenty-six single-letter phonograms plus forty-nine multi-letter phonograms consisting of two-letter digraphs, three-letter trigraphs, and four-letters quadgraphs. Different letter combination arrangements can make dramatically different sounds. For instance, the letter *C* can sound like /k/ or /s/ on its own but when it is combined to make *CI,* it will say /sh/. When *C* is combined with *H*, the *CH* makes the /ch/ sound, and when *C* links with *EI*, the *CEI* combined sound is /s/ /ē/, as in the word *ceiling*. Teaching children to connect each letter combination to its sound is the key to helping them become fluent readers and spellers.

In her book *Uncovering the Logic of English*, Denise Eide explains, "Learning the 75 basic phonograms is the true foundation for literacy and spelling. . . . They explain 98 percent of English words and are vital building blocks. . . . Students who

72

understand the 75 basic phonograms easily recognize advanced ones within words. Many of the advanced phonograms are related to the 75 basic phonograms." For instance, *-AIGH* is an advanced phonogram that makes the long /ā/ sound, but children may be able to read it if they know the basic phonogram—*AI* says long /ā/.

Although it will take most students time and practice to learn the seventy-five basic phonograms, the good news is that you can use the same four-step sequence each time you introduce a new sound:

FOUR STEP SEQUENCE FOR INTRODUCING SOUNDS

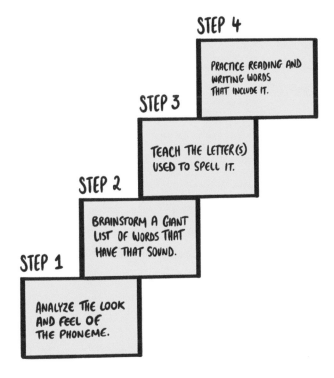

STEP 4
PRACTICE READING AND WRITING WORDS THAT INCLUDE IT.

STEP 3
TEACH THE LETTER(S) USED TO SPELL IT.

STEP 2
BRAINSTORM A GIANT LIST OF WORDS THAT HAVE THAT SOUND.

STEP 1
ANALYZE THE LOOK AND FEEL OF THE PHONEME.

Step 1: Analyze the look and feel of the phoneme.

Investigating the look and feel of a phoneme is a helpful first step because it launches the learning from children's spoken language superpower. Moving from what they already know (speech sounds) to what they are learning (the written letters that represent them) makes identifying the link easier.

Each speech sound has a unique recipe. As you and your students analyze sounds, point out how their mouths form a specific shape, their teeth move to a predictable position, their breath has a certain flow, etc. Helping children recognize every defining recipe takes the speech sounds from something they just do to something they can *intentionally* do. That conscious awareness helps form the neural pathways fluent readers use to quickly recall sounds while they are reading.

Handheld mirrors are useful with this step because students can easily see the shape and behavior of their mouths. Dollar stores often have enough mirrors in stock to purchase an entire class set.

The Science of Reading in Action

To analyze the look and feel of each speech sound, ask students five questions while they look in a handheld mirror:

1. What are your lips doing?
2. What are your teeth doing?
3. What is your tongue doing?
4. What is your voice box doing?
5. How is your air flowing?

As children pinpoint each answer, they will make exciting discoveries. For instance, when students focus on the short /ă/ sound in *apple,* they will see their lips open wide and round, their teeth will part, and their tongue will rest on the bottom of their mouth, lightly touching the back of their teeth.
When children place their fingertips against their voice box and say the sound again, they will feel the sound's vibration or lack of vibration.

And when they place their open palm in front of their mouth and feel for air, they will notice a gentle, breathy stream. It is amazing to realize that one simple sound has so many different characteristics!

Scan the QR code to watch a student work through these steps.

Students will notice a variety of attributes for each sound they learn. Several of the most distinguishing features include where the sound is made and whether the lips, teeth, and tongue are positioned in the front, middle, or back of the mouth. Sounds will also differ in **how** they are made—for instance, whether the airflow is blocked or unobstructed and whether it flows through the mouth or the nasal cavity. Sounds can even be distinguished by their voicing! When children say a "voiced" sound including /v/ or /m/, they will be able to feel their vocal cords vibrate by placing their fingers gently on their voice box. If they pronounce an "unvoiced" sound such as /f/ or /ch/, there will not be a vibration. Although it will be difficult for many children to recognize these defining characteristics at first, with practice they will become increasingly adept at noticing and describing each sound's unique features.

> **Step 2: Brainstorm a giant list of words with the phoneme.**

Brainstorming is always my favorite step of the process because it is fun to watch students' eyes grow wide as they realize how many words include the focus sound. For instance, short /ă/ is the first sound in *apple*, *ant*, *Adam*, and *astronaut*, but it also plays a part in the words *that, pancake, hand, ladder*, and so many more words.

Nothing motivates students to learn a letter–sound connection quite like realizing that they already say that sound thousands of times each day. Research shows that practicing spelling patterns within words (rather than as isolated rules) helps children learn more quickly and deeply.

To brainstorm the list, simply ask student volunteers to name all the words they can think of that include the focus sound and write each of the words on an anchor chart or whiteboard so everyone can see them. You can turn this into a motivating game by having students work with their neighbor and count the number of words they can think of together in just one minute. When the minute has passed, invite each pair to share a word so you can add it to the class list. No word is too short or too long—if it includes the focus sound, it counts.

Step 3: Teach the letters used to spell the sound.

After analyzing the phoneme and identifying words that include it, the next step is connecting the sound to the spellings. Research has proven that most children require an explicit explanation to make that connection. Our ultimate goal is for children to be able to switch written letters into sounds instantaneously, and that takes practice.

In this step, you'll circle the letters that created the sound you focused on in step two. Continuing the example above, you'll circle every letter (or letter combination) that creates the short /ă/

sound in your word list. Then ask students what they notice about the letters that were used to spell them. It won't take long for children to recognize that all of the short /ă/ phonemes are spelled by the letter A. From there, explicitly connect the letter and sound and then explain the letter and sound to connect the dots for any students who need an extra nudge by saying something like . . .

> The /ă/ sound is spelled with the letter A. Sometimes the A is written with an uppercase capital letter like this (write an A), and sometimes it is written with a shorter lowercase A that looks like this (write an a). What do you notice about the shapes of both of those As?

Some students might point out the straight lines of the uppercase *A* and the rounded circle of the lowercase version. Other children could notice that the capital *A* is taller than its shorter partner. All observations are valuable because they help the entire class notice defining characteristics that some students might otherwise miss.

After students share their discoveries, have them repeat the /a/ sound several times with you as you point to the pair of *As* to reinforce the letter–sound connection. Sound walls are a helpful tool for this step because they connect the look and feel of each sound to the letters that are used to spell them. Similar to word walls, sound walls are often displayed on bulletin boards so they can easily be seen from nearly every spot in the room. Unlike word walls, however, the bulletin board is filled with *sounds* instead of words.

Vowel sounds are displayed on a section of the wall called Vowel Valley. By definition, all vowel sounds have an unconstricted flow of air from the lungs. You can test this fact by trying to say the short /ŏ/ in octopus without releasing any air. It is impossible!

VOWEL VALLEY

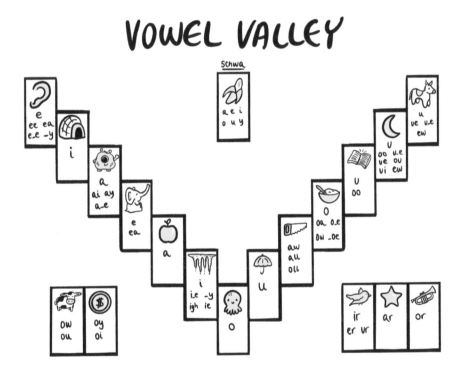

Another defining characteristic of vowels is that they are the stressed sound in a syllable. If you were to measure your audio levels when you said the word *cat,* you would see a peak when you pronounced the vowel /ă/. That audio peak is found in every syllable we say in English and is always made by the vowel sound.

The Science of Reading in Action

Although students learn to name the vowel *letters* quickly (*A, E, I, O, U,* and sometimes *Y*), it may be more of a struggle to recall all of the vowel *sounds* because there are so many of them. You will remember from Chapter Three that when you tally the long and short vowels, diphthongs, r-controlled vowels, and the most common vowel sound, *schwa*, there are eighteen different vowel sounds. (Mind-blowing, isn't it?)

All of these vowel sounds are organized on a sound wall based on the shape your mouth makes when the sound is made and the place where your sound is produced. If you are new to Vowel Valley, grab a mirror and watch your mouth as you say the sounds in order from left to right, starting with the long /ē/ sound. You will notice that the origin of the sound moves from front to back in your vocal cavity and high to low in your tongue position. The long /ē/ is made with smiling lips, and the sound comes from the front of your mouth while your tongue is high on your roof. As you say the sounds that follow, your tongue drops and your mouth becomes wider until you reach an open, low short /ŏ/ sound in the middle of the V. Working your way back up the other side of Vowel Valley, the next group of sounds is rounded and back— your tongue moves to the back of your mouth, and the sound comes from further back in your throat—and as these changes occur, your mouth closes.

The schwa /ə/ in the middle of Vowel Valley is sometimes referred to as the "lazy vowel" because your mouth barely opens when you say it. The letter *A* in *BALLOON* and the *E* in *PROBLEM* both make schwas because they sound like you are thinking: *uhhh.* All of the vowels can spell schwas, making it the most diverse sound in the bunch. Because it is considered a neutral sound, it lands smack-dab in the middle of Vowel Valley.

As you look at Vowel Valley, you may notice that most of the sounds can be spelled in a variety of ways. The long /ōō/ in *MOON*, for example, can be created with four different spellings: *U, OO, U_E*, or *UI*. Do not try to tackle all of these spelling patterns at once! Instead, focus on one at a time so children can really learn each one. Your instruction during step three may sound something like this:

> **TEACHER:** As you are looking at our giant list of long /ōō/ words, what do you notice about the letters we circled?
>
> **STUDENT:** There are a lot of different ways to spell that sound!
>
> **TEACHER**: Yes, you're right. In fact, the long /ōō/ can actually be spelled four different ways: *U, OO, U_E*, or *UI*. Today, we are going to focus on the OO spelling so we can help our brains learn it really well. We use the letters *OO* to make the long /ōō/ sound in words like *MOON, BOO, FOOD, HOOP, NOON, GOOF, BLOOM, ROOF, BOOT, SOON, COOL*, and *BOOM*. There are a lot of words that use *OO* to make their /ōō/ sound, aren't there? Let's practice spelling some of them together.

By paring down the list from four spellings to just one, children will be able to master the skill more easily and confidently than if they tried to tackle all the spellings at once. Circle back and focus on another spelling at a different time.

On the other side of the sound wall are all the consonant or non-vowel sounds. By definition, these sounds have a partial or total blockage of airflow. They can be sorted several different ways, but we will break them into six categories:

- **Stops:** Sounds made with a closed vocal tract. Air builds up and bursts out like in the sounds /p/ and /b/.
- **Nasals:** Sounds made by completely blocking airflow through your mouth and, instead, letting the air pass through your nose as in /m/ and /n/.
- **Fricatives**: Sounds made by partially blocking the vocal tract to force air through a narrow channel like the sounds /f/ and /v/.
- **Affricates:** Sounds that start as stops with air building up but end as fricatives when the air releases through a narrow channel. /Ch/ and /j/ are both affricates.
- **Glides:** Also called "semi-vowels," these sounds always come before vowels and seem to glide into the vowel sound, as in /wh/, /w/, and /y/.
- **Liquids**: Sounds that have slight air obstruction but not enough to cause any friction. /L/ and /r/ are liquids.

CONSONANTS

	LIPS TOGETHER	TEETH ON LIP	TONGUE BETWEEN TEETH	TONGUE BEHIND TOP TEETH	LIPS ROUND, TONGUE PULLED BACK	BACK OF TONGUE LIFTED	BACK OF THROAT
STOPS	P B			T -ed D -ed		G C K _CK CH	
NASALS	M			N gn kn		-ng -n-	
FRICATIVES		F ff ph V -ve	Th Th		Sh ti ci		H
AFFRICATES					CH _tch J -dge ge -gi gy		
GLIDES	Wh W				Y		
LIQUIDS				L -ll	R wr		Qu X

There are dozens of different opinions about the best order to teach consonant sounds, but no conclusive research exists. No matter the sequence, most experts agree that learning a few consonants and vowels early is what is most important. This allows children to begin reading and spelling words quickly. If you start by teaching the eight sounds /m/, /s/, /f/, short /ă/, /p/, /t/, /c/, and short /ĭ/, new readers will be able to read and spell hundreds of words, including *mat, pit, fast, spit, sat, past, mist,* and *tap.* Louisa Moats explains, "Systematic programs begin with a limited set of sound–symbol correspondences—a few consonants and one or two vowels—so that words can be built right away."

Once children learn individual letter sounds, you can move on to increasingly more complicated spelling and phonogram rules:

- **Digraphs:** two-letter pairs that make one sound, such as *SH* and *TH*
- **Blends:** two-letter pairs that are pronounced so quickly they seem to blend, such as *FR* and *SN*
- **Silent final E:** words ending with a silent *E*, as in *MAKE* and *GIVE*
- **Vowel teams:** two vowels that work together to make one sound, such as *AI* and *EA*
- **Diphthongs**: two vowels in a syllable that work together to make one sound, as in *FOIL* and *TOY*
- **R-influenced vowels:** a vowel that changes its sound because it is written next to R, such as the *IR* in *BIRD* and the *AR* in *CAR*

- **Word endings**: an additional part of a word that is added to a root, such as *ED* tacked onto *WALK* to make the new word *WALKED*
- **Contractions:** two words that are shortened and combined to make one word, such as when *CAN NOT* becomes *CAN'T*
- **Homophones:** identical sounds with different meanings, such as *TO, TWO*, and *TOO*

PHONICS ORDER

	GENERAL SKILL	NOTES
1	Letter sounds	Use the sound wall. Have students use a mirror to focus on the look and feel of each sound.
2	CVC short vowel word families	Focus on one vowel family at a time in this order: A, O, E, U and I.
3	Digraphs	Two letters that make just one sound
4	Blends	Two consonant sounds that are said so quickly that they almost blend together
5	Magic E	When a silent E is added to the end of a word, it makes the vowel say its name
6	Vowel teams	Two vowels that work together to make one sound.
7	Diphthongs	AKA "vowel digraphs" including OI, OO and AW
8	R-influenced vowels	The vowel sound changes when it is placed next to an R.
9	Word endings	For example, adding an –ED or –S to the end of a word
10	Contractions	For instance, can not becoming can't
11	Homophones	Homo = same Phone = sound

The Science of Reading in Action

Just as a cake grows taller by adding layers, students make progress by starting with basic letter sounds and adding new layers of phonics and spelling rule difficulty over time. Following this systematic order is a magical formula for goosebump-worthy reading growth!

On the next few pages I have included tables of basic phonograms. The sounds are arranged in order of frequency.

The Science of Reading in Action

BASIC PHONOGRAMS

Note: The sounds are arranged in order of frequency.

Phonogram	Phonemes (Speech sounds)	Examples	Spelling Rules & Notes
a	short /ă/ long /ā/ short /ŏ/	man bake father	A usually says its long sound at the end of a syllable.
ai	long /ā/	hair	
ar	/ar/	car	
augh	short /ă/ /f/ short /ŏ/	laugh caught	The phonograms AUGH, EIGH, IGH, OUGH are only used at the end of a base word or before T. The GH is either pronounced /f/ or is silent.
aw	short /ŏ/	draw	
ay	long /ā/	day	When a base word ends with a long /a/ sound, it is usually spelled AY.
b	/b/	bed	
bu	/b/	buy	
c	/k/ /s/	cat cereal	C says /k/ unless it is followed by the letters E, I, or Y.
cei	/s/ long /ē/	ceiling	
ch	/ch/ /k/ /sh/	check school chef	
ci	/sh/	glacier	This Latin /sh/ phonogram is only used at the beginning of syllables that come after the first one.
ck	/k/	deck	This phonogram is only used after a single short vowel.

The Science of Reading in Action

Phonogram	Phonemes (Speech sounds)	Examples	Spelling Rules & Notes
d	/d/	dog	
dge	/j/	ledge	This phonogram is only used after a single short vowel.
e	short /ĕ/ long /ē/	jet me	E usually says its long sound at the end of a syllable.
ea	long /ē/ short /ĕ/ long /ā/	heat breath great	
ear	/er/	learn	
ed	short /ĕ/ /d/ /d/ /t/	visited played danced	Add ED to the end of a verb to make it past tense unless it is an irregular verb. If the root word ends in T or D, the ED ending will say /ed/. If the root word ends with a voiced sound like /l/ or /m/, the ED ending will say /d/. If the root word ends in an unvoiced sound like /p/ or /k/, the ED will say /t/.
ee	long /ē/	keep	
ei	long /ā/ long /ē/ long /ī/	rein receipt feisty	
eigh	long /ā/ long /ī/	eight height	The phonograms AUGH, EIGH, IGH, OUGH are only used at the end of a base word or before T. The GH is either pronounced /f/ or is silent.

The Science of Reading in Action

Phonogram	Phonemes (Speech sounds)	Examples	Spelling Rules & Notes
er	/er/	nerd	
es	short /ĕ/ /z/ /z/	buses buzzes	To make a noun plural, add an ES if it ends in X, S, SH, or CH. For everything else, simply add S. —— Another way of saying the rule above is add an S unless it will make the word ending hiss.
ew	long /ōō/ long /ū/	chew few	
ey	long /ā/ long /ē/	they honey	
f	/f/	fish cliff	When /f/ /l/ or /s/ is heard after a short vowel at the end of a one syllable word, it is spelled with a double FF, LL, SS, or ZZ.
g	/g/ /j/	goat germ	G says /g/ unless it is followed by the letters E, I, or Y.
gn	/n/	gnome	
gu	/g/ /gw/	guess language	
h	/h/	ham	
i	short /ĭ/ long /ī/ long /ē/ /y/	in tiny stadium onion	I may say long /i/ when it is followed by two consonants. —— I may say long /e/ with a silent final E, at the end of a syllable, and at the end of international words.

89

Phonogram	Phonemes (Speech sounds)	Examples	Spelling Rules & Notes
ie	long /ē/	cookie	
igh	long /ī/	light	The phonograms AUGH, EIGH, IGH, OUGH are only used at the end of a base word or before T. The GH is either pronounced /f/ or is silent.
ir	/er/	bird	
j	/j/	jump	
k	/k/	kite	
kn	/n/	know	
l	/l/	leg doll	When /f/ /l/ or /s/ is heard after a short vowel at the end of a one syllable word, it is spelled with a double FF, LL, SS, or ZZ.
m	/m/	man	
n	/n/	nose	
ng	/ng/	song	
o	short /ŏ/ long /ō/ long /ōō/	off no to	O usually says its long sound at the end of a syllable. —— O may say long /o/ when it is followed by two consonants.
oa	long /ō/	boat	
oe	long /ō/ long /ōō/	toe shoe	

The Science of Reading in Action

Phonogram	Phonemes (Speech sounds)	Examples	Spelling Rules & Notes
oi	/oi/	foil	
oo	long /ōō/ short /ŏŏ/ long /ō/	school book floor	
or	long /ō/ /r/	born	
ou	/ow/ long /ō/ long /ōō/ short /ŭ/ short /ŏŏ/	cloud four soup country could	
ough	short /ŏ/ long /ō/ long /ōō/ /ow/ short /ŭ/ /f/ short /ŏ/ /f/	thought dough through plough tough cough	The phonograms AUGH, EIGH, IGH, OUGH are only used at the end of a base word or before T. The GH is either pronounced /f/ or is silent.
ow	/ow/ long /ō/	cow bow	
oy	/oi/	toy	
p	/p/	pin	
ph	/f/	photo	
qu	/kw/	queen	Q always needs a U so the U does not count as a vowel.
r	/r/	rip	
s	/s/ /z/	sit boss is	When /f/ /l/ or /s/ is heard after a short vowel at the end of a one syllable word, it is spelled with a double FF, LL, SS, or ZZ.

Phonogram	Phonemes (Speech sounds)	Examples	Spelling Rules & Notes
sh	/sh/	show	SH spells /sh/ at the beginning of a base word and at the end of a syllable.
si	/sh/ /zh/	session vision	This Latin /sh/ phonogram is only used at the beginning of syllables that come after the first one.
t	/t/	toe	
tch	/ch/	match	This phonogram is only used after a single short or broad vowel.
th	unvoiced /th/ voiced /th/	thin them	
ti	/sh/	caption	This Latin /sh/ phonogram is only used at the beginning of syllables that come after the first one.
u	short /ŭ/ long /ū/ long /ōō/ short /ŏŏ/	up use ruby put	U usually says its long sound at the end of a syllable.
ui	long /ōō/	suit	
ur	/er/	curl	
v	/v/	vest	
w	/w/	win	
wh	/wh/ with breath	why	
wor	/wer/	work	
wr	/r/	wrist	
x	/ks/ /z/	box xylophone	

The Science of Reading in Action

Phonogram	Phonemes (Speech sounds)	Examples	Spelling Rules & Notes
y	/y/ short /ĭ/ long /ī/ long /ē/	yes gym my crazy	When a single-syllable word ends in a single-vowel Y, it always says long /ī/. ___ Y only says long /e/ in an unstressed syllable at the end of a multisyllable word.
z	/z/	zap buzz	Z always spells /z/ at the beginning of a base word. ___ When /f/ /l/ or /s/ is heard after a short vowel at the end of a one syllable word, it is spelled with a double FF, LL, SS, or ZZ.

> **Step 4: Practice reading and writing words that include it.**

The saying is true: Practice makes perfect—especially when it comes to learning letter–sound connections. That is why it is so important to follow phonics lessons by having children put the skills into action. If you introduce the CH digraph, have children read text with CH words such as chat, chin, and chop. When you are working on the OP word family, give students a passage with the OP words pop, hop, and mop.

The term decodable passage refers to a text that students can sound out independently because they have learned all of the phonogram and spelling rules they need to do so successfully. You can use decodable passages to give students the tailored follow-up they need to practice different specific phonics families (CH words or TH words, etc.).

Even after they've learned these phonics families, children may experience productive struggle in the beginning. As with any new ability, it will take time and effort for students to apply their phonics skills at first, and their reading may be slow and strenuous. With continual practice, their fluency will build, and their momentum will increase. Soon, those same slow readers will be zipping through their decodable passages, reading longer, more complicated strings of letters with instant accuracy.

Whew! There you have it. Our magical four-step system is complete. By analyzing the look and feel of each phoneme, brainstorming a giant list of words that include that sound, teaching the letters used to spell it, and rounding out the lessons by reading and writing relevant words, you will help students' brains lay the letter–sound superhighways they need to become fluent readers.

Call to Action

1. Master the seventy-five basic phonograms! Scan the QR code to the right and print the phonogram cheat sheet for yourself and a file folder sound wall for each of your students.

SCAN ME

2. Share a photo of your file folder sound walls on social media along with the hashtag **#scienceofreadinginaction**, so other teachers can learn about the power of phonics too!

MY NOTES

Chapter Five: How to Teach Words Ten Times Faster

In a small school just outside of Raleigh, North Carolina, patience was running thin for a veteran first-grade teacher named Debbie. She had tried all the tools in her box of tricks—songs teaching sight word spellings, flashcards reinforcing rote memorization, and literacy centers trying to make learning at least a little bit fun for students along the way. No matter how many different strategies she tried, many of her first graders still struggled to memorize words. They could sing, read, and spell a word fifty different times, but it just would not stick. Each time they ran across it, her students would slowly sound the word out one letter at a time. Debbie was frustrated and emotionally drained.

Everything changed with one simple little teaching tweak she learned during my Reading Roadmap training. The technique she implemented helped her students memorize words ten times faster. Many of her first graders started learning new words in just four or five exposures. Debbie contacted me later and said, "It's *amazing!* The kids love doing it and their reading and writing abilities have skyrocketed!"

What was the magical solution? *Orthographic mapping*—also affectionately called sound mapping. It is the third and final skill in the word reading bucket.

THE HIGH LEVEL VIEW OF READING

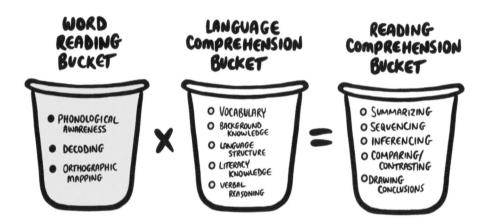

WORD READING BUCKET
- PHONOLOGICAL AWARENESS
- DECODING
- ORTHOGRAPHIC MAPPING

X

LANGUAGE COMPREHENSION BUCKET
- VOCABULARY
- BACKGROUND KNOWLEDGE
- LANGUAGE STRUCTURE
- LITERACY KNOWLEDGE
- VERBAL REASONING

=

READING COMPREHENSION BUCKET
- SUMMARIZING
- SEQUENCING
- INFERENCING
- COMPARING/CONTRASTING
- DRAWING CONCLUSIONS

For decades, many teachers (including me) believed that students memorized words by simply seeing them over and over again. However, if that were true, fluent readers would need to store tens of thousands of word pictures in their brains; that would require a lot of mental storage space! If those words were written in different fonts or with new capitalization? Lights out! Their brains would not be able to recognize the words in their new form. Humans simply do not have enough mental storage space to collect pictures of the millions of different ways every word might look. But if readers are not memorizing pictures of words by sight, what *are* they doing?

As a fluent reader, when you see a word, your brain instantly recognizes it because it has been stored in your brain's high-speed mental library called your *orthographic lexicon*. This library iis filled with thousands and thousands of mental file folders. Each folder contains either a word's spelling, pronunciation, or meaning. Your brain keeps them all organized in specific locations so that you can quickly find them anytime you need access.

Every word with a complete set of these lexicon file folders is called a sight word because your brain is able to quickly grab them off the shelves and combine the information together so you know the word's spelling, pronunciation, and meaning. But that term sight word may have a different definition than you've used in the past. I used to refer to sight words when I was talking about the long lists of Dolch or Fry high-frequency words I wanted my students to memorize each year. Literacy experts, however, use the term very differently. Sight words are not words you want students to memorize; they are words students have already memorized. Our teaching goal is for every student to have stored tens of thousands of instantly recognizable sight words so they can read with accuracy and fluency.

In 2005, Linnea Ehri published *Learning to Read Words* and explained, "If readers attempt to decode words, to analyze, or to predict words, their attention is shifted from the text to the word itself to identify it, and this disrupts comprehension, at least momentarily. It is clear that being able to read words automatically from memory is the most efficient, unobtrusive way to read words in text. Hence, building a sight vocabulary is essential for achieving text-reading skill."

Simply put, humans only have so much brain power available. When a new reader is using every ounce of mental capacity to sound out and blend the individual parts of words, they do not have enough space to also focus on what those words mean.

Until reading becomes more fluent and automatic, comprehension will be severely compromised. New readers will struggle to read a story on their own and be able to simultaneously reflect on what is happening. That is why we must help students memorize as many words as we possibly can so they can think more deeply about what they are reading and begin to enjoy the reading process.

The great news is that you can throw away all of your sight word flashcards and take down your word walls; you will never use them again. You will be able to teach students words significantly faster by using orthographic mapping. Instead of focusing on how words look, you will switch students' focus to how they *sound*.

Ortho means *correct*; *graphy* translates to *writing*; and *mapping* means to *connect the spelling, pronunciation*, and *meaning*. Put more simply, orthographic mapping is the process of organizing the spelling, pronunciation, and meaning of words in those handy folders in the brain's orthographic lexicon.

Take a moment to read these three words:

sting sling slink

Fluent readers can immediately read *sting, sling,* and *slink* even though just one letter differentiates the three spellings. *Sting* changed to *sling* by swapping the *T* for *L*. Sling switched to slink by making the G a K. It is amazing that the brain can instantly pick up on the minuscule differences and read similar but different words correctly.

To memorize a string of letters, it must have meaning. For instance, ASAP is very likely a meaningful letter string to you because it is an acronym for *as soon as possible*. When those same letters are organized in a different order like AASP or PAAS, they immediately lose their meaning and become unfamiliar. Even as a fluent reader, if I asked you to name those random letter sequences ten minutes from now, it's unlikely you would be successful because they are empty, meaningless letter strings. Your brain hasn't created a file folder for them.

This same concept applies to words students are trying to memorize! For letter sequences such as *are* and *the* to be stored in children's long-term memory, they need to have meaning. The best way to give those letter strings meaning is to connect the letters to the sounds they make. Students can then blend those sounds to form a complete word they already know.

Said a little differently, when a word's spelling is connected to its pronunciation and meaning, it automatically becomes a sight word. This is how fluent readers can instantly pronounce and make meaning of the 50,000 to 90,000 sight words they memorize over their lifetime. Instead of relying on visual processing, fluent readers build their orthographic lexicon around their oral language filing systems—the same systems they use to easily understand and communicate in verbal conversations.

The Magic of Sound Mapping

Although orthographic mapping might sound complicated, it is surprisingly simple to teach with a simple teaching tool called a sound map. (You can download this one a little later in this chapter.)

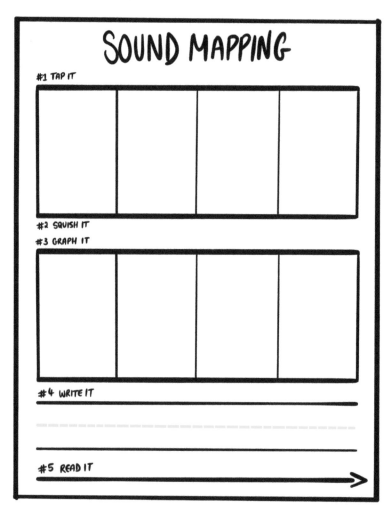

The tool is similar to the Elkonin Boxes described in Chapter Three. With the sound map tool, however, students will connect written letters to words' sounds. They will work their way through six steps that intentionally move from pulling apart individual phonemes to connecting each of those phonemes to their letters, and finally, to reading the entire word so they can recognize its meaning. No matter what word you are teaching, the sound map steps will always be the same: *tap it, map it, graph it, write it, read it,* and *repeat it.*

1. **Tap it**. After you say the word and have students repeat it back to you to confirm they are hearing the sounds correctly, have children use their fingers to tap the phonemes on the table or the palm of their other hand.

> **TEACHER:** Cat
> **STUDENTS:** Cat
>
> **STUDENTS:** /c/ (tap) /ă/ (tap) /t/ (tap)

2. **Map it.** Next, ask them to slide a manipulative like a counting chip or mini eraser into a box for each sound as they say the phonemes again.

> **STUDENTS:** /c/ (slide) /ă/ (slide) /t/ (slide)

3. **Graph it.** Have children write the letters they use to spell each phoneme while they repeat them.

> **STUDENTS:** /c/ (write C) /ă/ (write A) /t/ (write T)

4. **Write it.** Ask them to write the complete word on the line.

STUDENTS: /c/ (write C) /ă/ (write A) /t/ (write T)

5. **Read it.** Students will slide their fingers underneath the word as they blend the sounds.

STUDENTS: Cat (slide along the arrow)

6. **Repeat it.** Students will repeat the first five steps four more times to help their brains commit it to memory.

The Science of Reading in Action

Although this step-by-step run-through for the word cat is simple, words like said and the can seem a little more complicated; in fact, I often hear from teachers who need help understanding how to sound map those words. Let's work through both of those examples here so you are empowered to be successful. Remember, the six steps are always the same independent of the words you are practicing: tap it, map it, graph it, write it, read it, and repeat it.

Sound Map Steps	Students
1. Tap it.	TEACHER: Said STUDENTS: Said STUDENTS: /s/ (tap) /ĕ/ (tap) /d/ (tap)
2. Map it.	STUDENTS: /s/ (slide a chip) /ĕ/ (slide a chip) /d/ (slide a chip)
3. Graph it.	STUDENTS: /s/ (write S) /ĕ/ (write AI) /d/ (write D)
Note: If children don't immediately know that this short /ĕ/ sound is spelled with an AI, you can help them by having them erase the letters they initially wrote in that box and explain that the word SAID uses the letters AI to make the short /ĕ/ sound. After they have written the new letters in the box, have the children draw a heart next to them as a friendly reminder that they need to remember the AI spelling by heart.	
4. Write it.	STUDENTS: /s/ (write S) /ĕ/ (write AI) /d/ (write D)
5. Read it.	STUDENTS: Said (slide along the arrow)
6. Repeat it.	STUDENTS: (repeat steps 1 to 5 four more times)

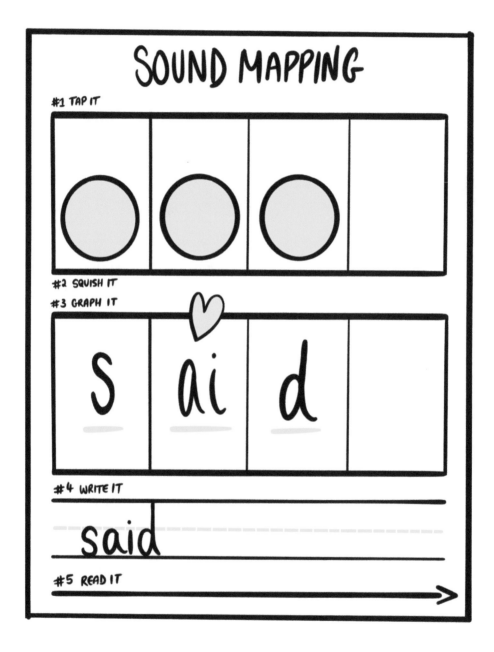

SOUND MAPPING

#1 TAP IT

#2 SQUISH IT

#3 GRAPH IT

s ai d

#4 WRITE IT

said

#5 READ IT

The Science of Reading in Action

Now let's work through the same six sound mapping steps for the.

Sound Map Steps	Students
1. Tap it.	TEACHER: The STUDENTS: The STUDENTS: /th/ (tap) /schwa ə/ (tap)
2. Map it.	STUDENTS: /th/ (slide a chip) /schwa ə/ (slide a chip)
3. Graph it.	STUDENTS: /th/ (write TH) /schwa ə/ (write E)
Note: If children initially struggle with the schwa ə, help them by explaining that the word the uses the letter E to make the /schwa ə/ sound. After they have written it in the box, have students draw a heart as a friendly reminder that they need to remember the E by heart.	
4. Write it.	STUDENTS: /th/ (write TH) /schwa ə/ (write E)
5. Read it.	STUDENTS: The (slide along the arrow)
6. Repeat it.	STUDENTS: (repeat steps 1 to 5 four more times)

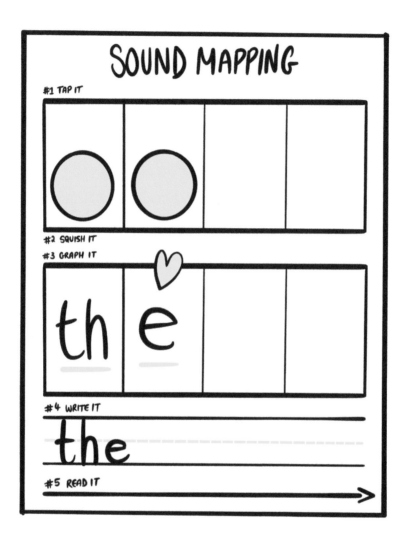

The steps are simple to implement, but the impact is significant. Good readers can memorize a new word in just one to five exposures when they connect a word's spelling, pronunciation, and meaning in one ready-to-retrieve mental file folder. Once a word is memorized, the word is never forgotten. Exciting, isn't it?

The Four Phases of Sight Word Development

When children begin memorizing sight words, they move through four distinct phases of development. The first one is called the *pre-alphabetic phase*, and it is typically brief. In this initial stage, children lack the letter–sound knowledge to be able to map words and add them to their permanent memory bank. To compensate, they store words based on how they look. For instance, they might remember the word stop when they see it on a sign or recognize *E* when it is written over a doorway exit, but if those words appeared in a newspaper or book, they would not know them.

The second stage of sight word development is called *partial alphabetic* because students can make some letter–sound connections. If they were reading the word *stop*, they might map the first and last sounds and then be able to recognize it later when they saw it again. If children saw a similarly spelled word like *step* or *shop*, they could easily misread it as *stop* because they only mapped part of the word.

With practice, children move to the third phase of sight word development, called *full alphabetic*. During this stage, children are able to map every sound in a word and, as a result, experience less confusion when they see similar spellings. In our previous example, students would correctly read *stop, step,* and *shop* because they could map each of their spellings, pronunciations, and meanings from start to finish.

In the last phase of sight word development, called

consolidated alphabetic, children begin grouping common letter patterns and sounds as units so they can map words more quickly and efficiently. If children have already mapped the words *night, right, fight,* and *sight*, for example, when they are shown the word *blight*, they would be able to read it by relying on the rime -IGHT.

Sounding out words in chunks rather than individual phonemes provides a noticeable leap in efficiency. Once students reach the consolidated alphabetic phase, the momentum of their reading fluency and accuracy snowballs. Children can learn new words on their own with increasing speed and precision because they are able to rely on the word units, spelling patterns, and phonics rules they already know. When they read words such as *basketball* or *computer*, they can break them into their syllables to make the words more manageable: bas—ket—ball and com—pu—ter.

No matter what stage students are in, one thing is clear: Fluent reading is not something that just happens. It is a skill that is intentionally taught and developed. Becoming a fluent reader requires learning a combination of phonological awareness, decoding, and orthographic mapping. With these tools, children can connect all of the dots they need to be able to successfully sound out words.

Call to Action

1. See the power of sound maps for yourself! Scan the QR code and print out your own set.

SCAN ME

2. Help spread the word about this game-changing tool by sharing a photo of your sound mapping station on social media along with the hashtag **#scienceofreadinginaction.**

MY NOTES

Chapter Six: Are Sight Word Lists Dead?

Before moving to the next bucket of reading skills, it is important to address the elephant in the room: sight word lists. In the previous chapter, we learned that flashcard drills are ineffective because they are based exclusively on visual memorization. It would be natural to assume that memorizing high-frequency sight word lists, such as Dolch and Fry, is a thing of the past. But that is not the whole story!

Many states and school districts *require* students to learn dozens of words from those lists each year. In fact, they are part of the Common Core Standards many classrooms use as benchmarks for student learning—and for good reason. If we want to empower children to become independent readers as quickly as possible, we need to work smarter, not harder. Although there are an estimated 600,000 words in the English language, a 2019 survey found that just thirteen account for 25 percent of all the words in a text. Researchers Jerry Johns and Kristine Wilke referred to those words as the "magic 13." They are: *a, and, for, he, in, is, it, of, that, the, to, was, you*.

Between 100 and 200 high-frequency words constitute more than 50 percent of reading material. Because children will see those same words over and over again, memorizing them provides significant time and sanity savings.

There is, however, a serious problem with sight word lists....

Because high-frequency sight word lists are organized by the number of times words appear in text, they ignore phonics and spelling rules completely. Students are forced to wrap their brains around very different skills at the same time, which can be confusing, overwhelming, and downright ineffective.

Picture a class of kindergarteners trying to memorize the following three words in the same week: *here, and*, *in*. Each word follows a vastly different phonics rule. To understand the word *here*, children need to learn about the role of silent *E*, but for the word *and*, students need to dive into the short /ă/. Never mind the short /ĭ/ that is part of the word *in*! Trying to learn all of these different phonics and spelling rules at the same time would be tough for anyone, let alone a brand-new reader who is just beginning to master letter–sound connections.

There are, however, clear benefits to teaching high-frequency words so children learn to recognize them right away. How can we solve this sight word dilemma? Here are three powerful solutions:

Solution #1: Reorganize Your List

Sort high-frequency words by spelling or phonics skills. When Dolch and Fry each created their lists in the 1900s, they tallied how many times they came across each word while they worked their way through a stack of books. The most common words, *the*, *and, are,* and *to,* were written at the top of the list. Less common words, including *did* and *get,* were placed at the bottom.

Their thinking was not entirely flawed; it makes sense that students would benefit from learning the most common words first to avoid having to sound them out over and over again. However, the order requires children to tackle multiple phonics and spelling skills at once. By reorganizing the high-frequency words by spelling and phonics, children can learn the words and the skill at the same time. Students can practice all of the short /ă/ words right alongside a short /ă/ phonics lesson. Then, when they are ready to move on to a new skill, readers can tackle the short /ĭ/ words. It is a simple tweak, but the change has a profound impact on students' learning.

When you sort your list by phonics and spelling skills, you will notice that words often fit in multiple categories. The word *them,* for example, could be taught with a lesson on the digraph /th/ or instruction on the short /ĕ/. I recommend teaching the word when you cover its most advanced skill so that children are learning just one new lesson instead of two. In this case, students will learn the short /ĕ/ first, so you would wait to work on *them* until they tackled the digraph /th/. Similarly, with the word *over,* instead of introducing it with other long /ō/ words, you would wait until you teach the *r*-controlled vowel /er/ because children will learn that skill later.

Look at the table of Dolch words to see how the first 133 high-frequency words can be reorganized based on phonics and spelling rules.

FIRST 133 DOLCH WORDS SORTED BY PHONICS AND SPELLING SKILLS

(Pre-kindergarten, Kindergarten, and First-Grade Dolch Words)

Short A Words	Short E Words	Short I Words	Short O Words	Short U Words	Schwa	TH Digraph	WH Digraph
am	red	in	on	up	the	that	when
at	get	is	not	but	of	this	what
an	yes	it	stop	run	from	them	
as	let	big		just	some	then	
and	help	him		must	again	with	
ask	went	his		jump	was		
can		did			away	CK Digraph	Silent E Words
ran		think				black	have
had							give
has							live
							come

Long A Words	Long E Words	Long I Words	Long O Words	Long U Words	R-Controlled	Diphthong Words	Double Letters
a	me	I	go	blue	her		will
say	we	like	no	you	over		well
may	be	ride	so	put	were		yellow
play	he	white	for		under		little
ate	see	find	old		after		pretty
came	she	my	open		every		funny
take	eat	by	going		four		all
make	three	fly			are		
thank	here						
they	please						
where							
there							

Diphthong Words					Other Rules
now	new	look	do	to	want
how	our	good	into	too	walk
down	out	saw	who	two	once
brown	round	to	soon	know	one
					said

Solution #2: Throw Out Flashcards

If your teaching experience has been anything like mine, you probably spent years printing and cutting apart sight word flashcards. Now that research has identified more effective ways to teach, you can swap those flashcards for the Sound Map tool you grabbed in the last chapter.

David Kilpatrick explains that helping children connect pronunciation, spelling, and meaning instead of relying on inefficient visual memory makes it possible for them to memorize a word in just one to five exposures. Compare that with the dozens and dozens of times most students need to see a flashcard before memorizing the word, and the choice becomes crystal clear: We can say goodbye to those time-consuming sight word drills once and for all.

Solution #3: Swap Leveled Readers for Decodable Readers

There are a variety of different book-leveling systems, but three of the most popular are Fountas and Pinnell, Lexile, and Daily Reading Assessment (DRA). Each one scores text difficulty based on an assessment of factors including the complexity of the vocabulary, the number of words on a page, and children's ability to predict unfamiliar words by looking at the illustrations and repetitive text. None of those leveling systems, however, uses phonics and spelling rules as part of their evaluation. As a result, books are often filled with words containing a huge range of skills, and it can be challenging for teachers to create a connection between reading lessons and the follow-up practice used for reinforcement.

Decodable readers, however, concentrate on a large number of phonetically similar words. One passage might be filled with words ending in the -AM rime and another decodable could be written with words that start with SH-. When Linnea Ehri shared findings from the National Reading Panel in 2003, she highlighted, "It is essential for students to be able to apply their alphabetic and word reading skills to the reading of stories. Systematic phonics programs typically provide special texts for this purpose. The texts are written so that most words are regularly spelled and contain the letter–sound correspondences that children have been taught up to that point. For example, in a text at the easiest level, a large number of words might contain the short /ă/ vowel. At a higher level, all the short vowels might appear in different words. At a still higher level, several long as well as short vowels would be present."

The systematic progression of skills employed by decodable readers allows students to apply their learning without relying on picture cues and guessing. (You can try them out for yourself in the action steps below.)

Are sight word lists dead? No, they serve an important role in the reading process when used effectively. But these three teaching tweaks turn those lists from problematic to invaluable. That's a big win in my book. (Pun intended!)

Call to Action

1. Scan the QR code to grab a set of short /ă/ decodable passages you can use right away.

SCAN ME

2. Share a photo of your new passages on social media so you can inspire other teachers to make the switch too.

#scienceofreadinginaction

Chapter Seven: Building Powerhouse Language Comprehension

Up to this point, we have been focused on the first bucket in the Simple View of Reading and have been building students' phonological awareness, decoding, and orthographic mapping so they can read the words on a page. Now we are going to dive into new territory and strengthen students' language comprehension so they can *understand* the words they are reading. Without this comprehension, there is no purpose in reading!

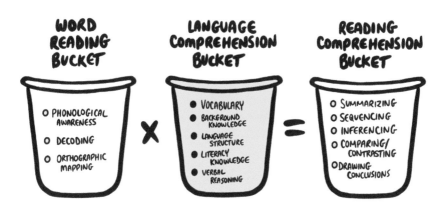

THE HIGH LEVEL VIEW OF READING

WORD READING BUCKET

O PHONOLOGICAL AWARENESS

O DECODING

O ORTHOGRAPHIC MAPPING

X

LANGUAGE COMPREHENSION BUCKET

● VOCABULARY
● BACKGROUND KNOWLEDGE
● LANGUAGE STRUCTURE
● LITERACY KNOWLEDGE
● VERBAL REASONING

=

READING COMPREHENSION BUCKET

O SUMMARIZING
O SEQUENCING
O INFERENCING
O COMPARING/ CONTRASTING
O DRAWING CONCLUSIONS

The Science of Reading in Action

To illustrate the difference between word reading and language comprehension, let's pull on our astronaut suits and blast off to a faraway planet called Blork. As our rocket ship touches down, we are greeted by an alien who hands us a paper with this extremely important message: DRAM PLID RO DOOB HOAT FEAM.

Because you are a fluent reader, I am confident that you can sound out all of the words. And yet, if I asked you what the urgent message says, you would be lost. It could be, "Congratulations! You are the new ruler of our planet," or it might say, "Leave immediately or we will attack." Without comprehension, the Blorkian words have no meaning; they are just a string of random letters temporarily floating through our brains. You'll have forgotten their exact order in a matter of minutes because meaning is what anchors words in your mind.

The skill that makes any string of letters stick is language comprehension. That's true for you and for your learners.

If a child spends three days reading all of the intergalactic, space-age chapters in *Star Wars* but is unable to tell you anything that happened in the story after he finishes the last page, he will have missed out on hours and hours of entertainment. Language comprehension is what makes stories enjoyable and books like this one educational. It involves three different brain tasks: phonological processing, meaning processing, and context processing.

3 BRAIN PROCESSES OF LANGUAGE COMPREHENSION

PHONOLOGICAL PROCESSING

LISTENING FOR AND PRODUCING SPEECH SOUNDS

MEANING PROCESSING

RETRIEVING EVERY MEANING STORED FOR THE WORD

CONTEXT PROCESSING

USING BACKGROUND KNOWLEDGE AND LARGER CONTEXT TO DECIDE WHAT MEANING FITS BEST

First, students need to be able to listen for and produce speech sounds. This begins with the building blocks of *phonological awareness* that we've discussed in the past few chapters, but it doesn't end there. When children have the opportunity to talk with each other through class discussions, think-pair-shares, and group projects, they stretch their *phonological processing* abilities too. The words you use to communicate and the unique way you pronounce specific speech sounds can be different from those of your students. Their families may have raised them with other regional accents or may have introduced them to unique phrases. It is important to take full advantage of that diversity to deepen children's phonological processing.

Language comprehension also involves *meaning processing*. Going back to the note from the Blork alien, comprehension was the missing piece.

To process the meaning of words, your brain retrieves every definition it has stored for a word. Those meanings are organized in a variety of ways, including synonym relationships, roots and other morphemes, spelling patterns, and shared meanings. Because of these multiple layers of connections, it is helpful for students to learn new vocabulary in relation to other known words so they can make connections based on their similarities and differences.

When you saw the alien message, you did not have a single stored meaning for any one of those words. You could not pull meaning from a comparably spelled word or take an educated guess based on a word root. Although you could phonologically process and pronounce the speech sounds, you could not connect those sounds to any possible meanings.

This speech processing without comprehension is exactly what many English Language Learners experience in class every day! They hear people speaking around them and may be able to process the sounds phonologically, but until they are able to take the next step and connect those sounds to meanings, they will be unable to comprehend the conversation. Consequently, they will also struggle with the third and final piece of the language comprehension pie: context processing.

Context processing occurs when you use your background knowledge and the larger understanding of the situation to decide which meaning best fits a word. For instance, the statement "I grabbed chips today," could mean a wide variety of different things. You will need to use your background knowledge and the larger context to pinpoint the intended message. If we are talking about our dinner plans and you know I love nachos, you could conclude that the word chips refers to tortilla chips. But if we are talking about garden projects and you know I plan on freshening up my garden beds, you would naturally determine that chips means wood chips. The same sentence can have very different meanings depending on the background knowledge and larger context.

THE LANGUAGE PROCESSING SYSTEMS

Name of System	Function	Example
Phonological Processing	Hears and processes a word.	Your friend says, "I broke my nail." Your brain hears *nail* and then activates the *meaning* processing system.
Meaning Processing	Retrieves every stored meaning for the word.	You pull out all of your stored meanings for *nail*:small metal spike,finger and toe covering,attaching something to a surface,tackling someone in a sports game, and acing a test. Then the context processing system is activated.
Context Processing	Use the background knowledge, context of the situation, and language structure to select the best meaning from the available options.	Your brain makes its best guess about the intended meaning and assumes your friend chipped her fingernail. When she explains that she was hitting it with a hammer to secure a roof shingle, your context processing system reevaluates and determines that she must be referring to a small metal spike.

All three of these brain processes are connected by neural pathways in the brain. Because spoken language is a human superpower, most students will be able to build their language comprehension quickly and with minimal effort. You can spur the development of this skill by providing plenty of opportunities for children to speak to each other through class discussions, think-pair-shares, and small group projects so they can practice comprehending and producing spoken language. Include diverse books in your read-aloud lineup to expose children to a variety of communication styles and vocabulary. Likewise, you can play audiobooks so students learn to pick out speech sounds with other speakers' accents and pronunciations.

As children practice, they will use all three of these processes to strengthen five key skills included in the language comprehension bucket:

1. Vocabulary
2. Background knowledge
3. Language structure
4. Literacy knowledge
5. Verbal reasoning

Vocabulary

Vocabulary is the understanding of the meaning of words. If you are brainstorming a list of *nocturnal* animals, your students need to know that nocturnal is an umbrella term for creatures that are active at night. Without that vocabulary knowledge, children will be unclear about what commonality connects the bats, owls, and raccoons on the list.

Take a moment to consider the very different experiences between linguistically advantaged and less-advantaged kindergarteners during your nocturnal animal unit. A child who previously learned words such as den, cave, predator, and prey will naturally have an easier time mastering the content than their peer who is hearing all of those terms for the first time.

When you stretch that example out across a full school day that is filled with dozens of other lessons and conversations, it is easy to understand why children entering kindergarten with a smaller toolbox of vocabulary terms naturally have a steeper learning curve.

How can you help those struggling students catch up? The simplest way to build children's vocabulary is to introduce them to new words and clearly define those words. In pre-kindergarten through second grade, most of that teaching happens verbally. To introduce the term *nocturnal*, you might say something like this:

> *Nocturnal* means things that are active at night. For instance, owls hunt, fly, and eat at night. Owls are nocturnal because they are moving around when it is dark outside. You are not active at night—you are sleeping—so you are not nocturnal.

As students learn to read more fluently, they will be able to build their vocabulary not just through spoken language but also while they are reading. Children will learn new scientific terminology from books on photosynthesis and outer space and will add to their repertoire of cultural terms when they study stories from around the world.

Background Knowledge

Background knowledge is the next language comprehension skill, and it refers to a student's prior understanding of concepts, situations, and problems. For example, let's pretend you have two children sitting side-by-side during your nocturnal animal discussion.

One student has gone on dozens of overnight camping trips with her family. She is able to pull from a treasure trove of nighttime experiences spent out in the wilderness and can confidently name many nocturnal animals. The other student, however, has never slept away from his home and is deeply fearful of the dark. He has almost no outdoor experiences at night and cannot contribute any nocturnal animals to the list. Although both children may understand what the word *nocturnal* means, their brainstorming participation will likely be vastly different simply because of their unmatched past experiences.

As their teacher, you can set your students up for success by anticipating the background knowledge they need and then providing it ahead of time. Before the nocturnal animal brainstorm, you might tell the class a story about a recent camping trip you took and describe the animal sounds you heard while you were falling asleep each night. Or in the days before your brainstorming activity, you could read stories about bats, owls, and raccoons so children could learn about their nighttime activity.

Language Structure

Language structure is the next language comprehension skill, and it means knowing how the arrangement of words within sentences impacts their meaning.

The word dress, for example, means something different when you say "I dress" compared with "I wear a dress." In the first case, dress is a verb—you are referring to the act of putting on clothes —but you could be zipping up a warm winter coat or pulling on a pair of socks.

In the second sentence, however, you are referring to a specific type of clothing, and dress is a noun. The only type of clothing you could be pulling on is a one-piece garment.

Although the word dress is pronounced and spelled the same, its position in the sentence and the words that surround it greatly affect its meaning. In fact, we could extend our list of possible dress definitions by working through sentences such as "I dress the turkey" and "Please dress the room with wallpaper."

When you multiply this simple dress example with thousands of similar examples we could work through, it quickly becomes clear why language structure is such an important part of children's language comprehension.

How can you teach language structure? When situations like this dress example present themselves, talk through the possible meanings with students. You can even act them out or have children draw a quick sketch showing the word's different possibilities. Fill-in-the-blank stories are also a fun way to learn about and practice parts of speech. To play, students must fill in missing words from a story by naming specific word types: nouns, verbs, adjectives, and adverbs. Children get excited to brainstorm parts of speech when they know their hard work will be rewarded with a humorous story at the end.

Literacy Knowledge

Literacy knowledge covers the language comprehension skills children use to read, write, and speak, including understanding how letters make words, words make sentences, and sentences make paragraphs, reading left to right across a page, and understanding the difference between a fiction and a nonfiction book.

One of the best ways to build literacy knowledge is a strategy called *thinking out loud*. During a read-aloud, pick a literacy knowledge skill you would like to focus on and explain how you are doing it. Your specific explanation gives students insight into simple actions that can otherwise seem mysterious. For instance, if you were teaching children about directional tracking so they understood the need to read and write English from left to right, you might introduce the lesson like this:

> Usually, when I read a story out loud to you, I just read the words in the book, but today I am going to do something extra special! I am going to open up my brain and tell you what it is doing so that you can do it when you read too.
>
> Today, we will focus on reading left to right across the page. Every time I start reading a new page, I always look at the first word on the left here. (Point to the top word on the left.)
>
> The very next word I read is the one written next to it. (Move your finger to the next word in the sentence.)

I keep reading the words across the line like this. (Slide your finger along until you reach the last word in that line.)

Then, when I get to the last word in a line, I move down to the next line of words and start on the left side again so that I can read from left to right across the page. (Slide your finger along several lines of text so that children can see the left-to-right motion you are repeating.)

I am going to read this entire page out loud and I want you to watch my pointer finger as I do it. You will notice that each time I start reading a new line of words, I jump back to the left side of the page and slide right.

Thinking out loud helps children learn what fluent readers are unconsciously doing while they read. Instead of leaving students to figure it out themselves, you are empowering them to put the skills into practice immediately.

Verbal Reasoning

Finally, verbal reasoning is the ability to decipher the deeper meaning of words, including similes, metaphors, and figures of speech. This skill is especially challenging for English Language Learners, but it can be difficult for native English speakers too. Unless deeper meanings are called out and explained, they can easily be missed.

For instance, if you say, "it is raining cats and dogs,"

immediately follow up by clarifying that it is raining hard. When you describe someone who is "as brave as a lion" or talk about how "opportunity is knocking at the door," tell children your intended meaning so they can grasp what you are trying to communicate.

COMMON ENGLISH IDIOMS

Idiom	Example Sentence	Intended Meaning
At the drop of a hat	I will come and pick you up at the drop of a hat.	To do something without hesitation
Beat around the bush	Please don't beat around the bush anymore. What's bothering you?	To avoid a difficult conversation
Cut corners	Don't cut corners! We want to do this right the first time.	To take a shortcut that will likely result in poorer quality
Cut the mustard	Unless you fix that, it's not going to cut the mustard.	To meet an acceptable standard of quality
Hang in there	I know it's hard but hang in there.	Continue persevering through the hardship
Hit the nail on the head	Your speech really hit the nail on the head.	To be completely accurate
It takes two to tango.	I know you're angry at him, but it takes two to tango.	Both people are at fault.
On the ball	Their news reports are always on the ball.	Doing well at an activity
Piece of cake	Winning that game was a piece of cake.	Something that is easy
Speak of the devil.	Speak of the devil! Look who just arrived.	The person who was just being discussed arrives.

Take that with a grain of salt.	He said you don't need to follow that rule, but I would take his advice with a grain of salt.	A warning not to take something seriously
Twist my arm	You don't have to twist my arm to cook you dinner.	To force someone to do something. It is usually used as a joke.
Under the weather	I am too ill to come to work today. I am really under the weather.	Feeling sick

By clearly connecting the dots rather than leaving children to link together connections on their own, you will not only ensure they learn the intended messages but you will also help them grow their verbal reasoning skills more quickly. Growing speed and accuracy is a double teaching win!

Call to Action

1. Pick an upcoming lesson and take a few minutes to brainstorm the vocabulary words and phrases that might be unfamiliar to students. Begin frontloading the vocabulary several days before the lesson so children have an initial exposure to it. Then, when you teach the lesson later, intentionally take time to explain the words so you can help set all of your students up for success (especially those who are less linguistically advantaged).

2. Share one of your recent teaching wins on social media, so other teachers can learn from it too.

Use the hashtag **#scienceofreadinginaction**

Chapter Eight: Crossing the Finish Line to Comprehension

"To learn to read is to light a fire; every syllable that is spelled out is a spark." - Victor Hugo

For years, I thought teaching reading comprehension was as simple as asking a few questions during read-aloud stories: *Who was the main character? What happened in the beginning, middle, and end of the story? How does this connect to your own life?* Boy, was I wrong!

As we have explored, comprehension is tied to a student's word reading and language skills. If a child's word reading is weak, he will be unable to sound out the words on a page. If he struggles with language comprehension, the words he reads will have no meaning. A child with a weakness in either skillset will have compromised reading comprehension too.

Reading comprehension is our next area of focus. As we shift to the results side of the Simple View of Reading equation, we are making the leap from spoken language comprehension to written language comprehension.

THE HIGH LEVEL VIEW OF READING

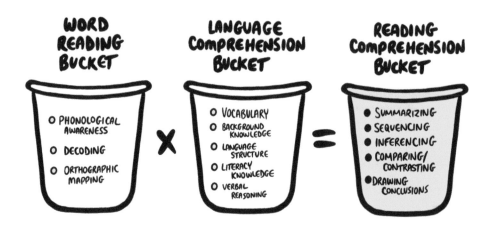

As noted in the previous chapter, the brain processes involved in verbal comprehension include three different skills: phonological processing, meaning processing, and context processing.

All three of those processes are also involved in reading comprehension. But there is also one additional skill activated in this stage: orthographic processing. Orthographic processing means translating words on the page to the spoken language we hear in our head.

4 BRAIN PROCESSES
OF READING COMPREHENSION

PHONOLOGICAL PROCESSING **MEANING PROCESSING** **CONTEXT PROCESSING** **ORTHOGRAPHIC PROCESSING**

TRANSLATING WORDS ON A PAGE TO SPOKEN LANGUAGE SO WE CAN HEAR THEM IN OUR HEAD.

Explained another way, the difference between language comprehension and reading comprehension is that students are transforming the words they see on paper into words they hear being read in their brain like an audiobook. The faster that change happens, the more skilled students' reading becomes.

Reading comprehension empowers students to understand and apply what they are reading. It is the key to summarizing, sequencing, making inferences, comparing texts, and drawing conclusions about an author's deeper meaning.

As children move from the primary grades to the intermediate level, holes in their reading comprehension and fluency can seem to pop up out of nowhere. A student may have aced their reading comprehension year after year but then *bam*! Suddenly, their comprehension stalls.

The Science of Reading in Action

It can be tempting to think that the problem is new, but it has usually existed all along. In the primary grades, students read simpler books with basic words such as *that, he*, and *my*. Consequently, holes in their language comprehension can go unnoticed. As soon as students start reading more complicated text involving advanced vocabulary, such as *solar energy* and *nocturnal animals*, weaknesses become glaringly clear. The LETRS training explains, "Language facility gained in earlier grades will have a major impact on reading comprehension in the intermediate grades and beyond." As students read increasingly complicated text, the strength of their spoken language comprehension skills becomes even more important for their success.

Historically, classroom observations found that reading comprehension skills were assessed but rarely taught. Today, however, we can draw on decades of scientific research that pinpoints the specific strategies that correspond to strong reading comprehension. When we teach students those skills, they learn to apply them in the following ways:

- Use personal background knowledge and opinions to make connections with the text.
- Monitor and adjust the pace and purpose of their reading.
- Mentally organize the information they gather.
- Draw from a strong general and specific vocabulary.

Many of these skills are invisible because they happen mentally. One of the most important research findings concludes, however, that clear instruction can accelerate learning growth. In their review of comprehension research studies, David Pearson and Margaret Gallagher summarize, "training either in strategy use or monitoring is beneficial, often to the lower achievers but more often to all students."

With these strong reading comprehension strategies in place, children are empowered to make mental models as they read. Their short- and long-term memory process the text's deeper meanings, feelings, images, and concepts and creates a rich understanding of what is happening. Because you have strong reading comprehension, if your friend asks you about Chapter Nine in this book, you will not remember the precise wording from every page, but you *will* be able to share highlights of the concepts and ideas. Those ideas are the mental models you use to summarize, predict, and analyze text.

The goal is to equip *all* students to develop that same ability. For young readers, you can help grow their mental dictionaries and background knowledge by practicing reading comprehension skills during read-aloud stories. Include challenging vocabulary words, diverse texts, and figures of speech in your lessons. Small teaching decisions will lead to big learning gains over time. Every breadcrumb you drop throughout the year will help students strengthen their *spoken* language comprehension, which, in turn, will bolster their *written* reading comprehension.

Call to Action

1. Now that you know reading comprehension is more than just sprinkling read-aloud stories with a few questions, fill in this blank: Reading comprehension is _____.

2. Share your answer on social media to help other teachers make discoveries about reading comprehension too.

Use the hashtag
#scienceofreadinginaction

Chapter Nine: Your Biggest Questions Answered

"The greatest gift is a passion for reading."
- Elizabeth Hardwick

I could geek out on best teaching practices and the science of reading findings for days and never grow tired of it, so it is probably no surprise that I get excited to chat with teachers about reading in my Instagram DMs and on other social media.

Since I often get asked the same questions over and over again, I am excited to share the answers, in anticipation of you wondering about them too. As I've discussed in earlier chapters, reading involves complex brain activities and, although it's important to understand the learning process at a high level, it is also necessary to know answers to more detailed questions so you can successfully implement both the science and art of reading. That is what this chapter is all about—nailing down must-know answers for your must-ask questions.

The Science of Reading in Action

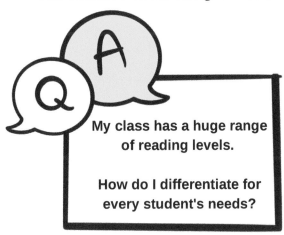

My class has a huge range of reading levels.

How do I differentiate for every student's needs?

I am so glad you asked because differentiation is a key to big reading growth! When students' specific strengths and needs are met, they are able to make significantly more progress. Just as a fluent reader would be bored to tears working on rhyming and syllable segmenting, a brand-new reader would be overwhelmed if you asked him to read a long historical novel. Every child must receive his or her just-right practice.

If you are like many teachers I chat with, your classroom is filled with a large range of reading abilities, and it may seem daunting to try and meet all of those needs at the same time. After all, you do not have 20,000 hours to plan, prep, and teach each day.

But luckily, even in a classroom with a big variety of learners, there are patterns. One cluster of students needs to work on basic letter sounds while another group is ready to dive into digraphs. Sorting children into small groups based on similar needs allows you to whittle your planning list down from twenty-five customized lessons to just three or four small group lessons.

I have a whole module showing you how to set up and run differentiated small groups inside The Reading Roadmap PD, but I hope this big-picture overview is a helpful start.

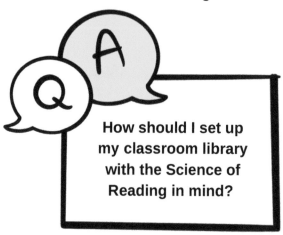

How should I set up my classroom library with the Science of Reading in mind?

Ooooh! Fabulous question. When I started teaching back in 2003, I was encouraged to organize my classroom library into two sections:

1. Sort all leveled books into bins based on their Developmental Reading Assessment score (level 1, level 2, etc.)
2. Sort all other books by topic (dinosaurs, back-to-school, etc.)

Here's the crazy news: Reading research has completely debunked that first category of leveled books. Studies have proven that leaning on predictable sentences and picture clues does not significantly improve students' reading. We now know that the Developmental Reading Assessment system I used to sort my bins does not meaningfully correspond to children's reading ability at all.

I've replaced leveled readers with decodable texts that require children to apply the phonics and spelling rules they have learned. This provides a systematic progression based on increasingly difficult skills.

What does that mean for your classroom library? The number 1 way to align it with the science of reading is to replace your leveled books with decodable ones. Instead of filling bins based on level, sort them by phonics skill. Have a bin of short /ă/ books and another box for short /ĕ/. With a quick swap and a little bit of organization, you'll make it easy for children to find a book practicing *their* just-right skills.

The Science of Reading in Action

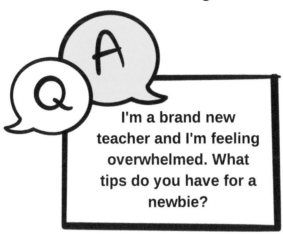

I'm a brand new teacher and I'm feeling overwhelmed. What tips do you have for a newbie?

I remember those first years of teaching so clearly. Every day is exciting and overwhelming at the same time. Please know that I am cheering you on from afar. I promise it gets easier!

As far as suggestions go, I don't know who said it first, but I love the advice "go slow to go fast." Especially when it comes to reading instruction, it can be tempting to want to jump into all the things right away: daily phonological awareness warmups, differentiated small group lessons, classroom library updates, etc.

The reality is that each one of those pieces takes time, tweaking, and optimizing to get right. If you try to perfect all of those lessons and activities at the same time, it will take a lot longer to find your groove. But if you focus on one thing you are excited to improve and put all of your efforts into mastering it, your momentum will take off like wildfire!

Giving ourselves grace is so important in all of this work. Students do not need perfect teachers; they need teachers who are committed to continually learning and growing for their benefit.

Please always feel free to reach out to me if there's anything I can do on my end to support you along the way!

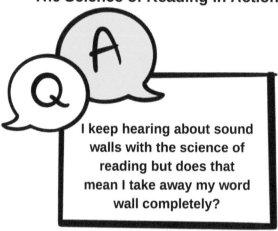

I keep hearing about sound walls with the science of reading but does that mean I take away my word wall completely?

Yes, you are correct! Sound walls replace word walls completely. Here's why:

Students learn words faster when they focus on the sounds they make instead of just trying to memorize how they look. Word walls take up a huge amount of space on classroom walls, and yet, they are almost entirely a visual tool. Each word is displayed as a reminder of what the spelling looks like.

Sound walls, on the other hand, help children focus on the letter–sound connections they need to learn to successfully read and spell. For instance, once children learn the eight sounds /m/, /s/, /f/, short /ă/, /p/, /t/, /c/, and short /ĭ/, they are empowered to read and spell hundreds of words, including fast, pit, sat, cast, fit, tap, and Sam. Sound walls are a much better use of your prime classroom real estate.

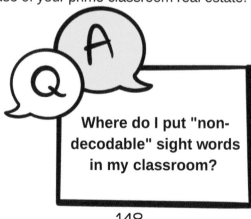

Where do I put "non-decodable" sight words in my classroom?

The Science of Reading in Action

I am excited that you asked this question because I have great news! Most words are decodable once you know the phonogram and spelling rules behind them. For instance, the word have might seem like a rule-breaker word if we think the silent E's only job is to make the vowel before it say its name; in fact, the silent E has seven different jobs, and one of them is preventing a V from being the last letter in a word. Once we know that rule, have is suddenly not an undecodable word after all.

The 7 Jobs of Silent E

1. A silent final E makes the vowel before it say its long sound: make, bite, pole, cube.
2. English words cannot end in the letters V or U, so E may be added: have, give, blue, clue.
3. A silent final E makes a C say /s/ and the G say /j/: face, ice, huge, age.
4. Every syllable must have a written vowel, so E is added when a syllable has just an L: little, turtle, waffle, google.
5. A silent E keeps singular words that end in S from being mistaken as plural: moose, purse, goose, house.
6. A silent E makes TH say its voiced sound: bath versus bathe, cloth versus clothe.
7. E is added to help distinguish between similar words: by versus bye, or versus ore.

Note: Sometimes an E is added for unknown reasons, as in done, come, were, and where.

The other fun news is that research has shown students do not memorize words based on their appearance. That means you no longer need to hang up word walls or have students drill a pile of sight word flashcards. Instead, you can save time and energy by having children sound map! It's a surprisingly simple teaching tweak that has an incredibly profound impact on students' learning.

The Science of Reading in Action

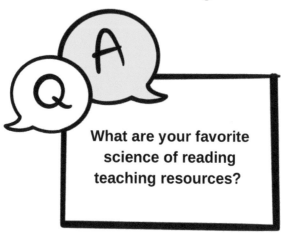

What are your favorite science of reading teaching resources?

Oh boy! I have a lot of them. If I were forced to narrow down my list, I'd pick four:

1. **Phonological awareness** daily warmups make it so easy to add consistent practice into your school day, and daily reinforcement works wonders for students' reading fluency.

2. **Sound walls** help children make important letter–sound connections. I love using them in combination with the phonogram chart because it explains spelling rules. For instance, if you are learning about the /c/ phonogram, you can quickly see it has two different sounds: /k/ and /s/. The phonogram chart explains that C will say /k/ unless it is followed by the letters E, I, or Y. With that quick and simple explanation, C suddenly loses its mystery, and students can use it correctly in their reading and spelling.

3. **Sound maps** help children memorize words in just one to five exposures. It still blows me away what a difference it makes to have students focus on the sounds they hear in words instead of on how they look. Sound maps are truly game-changing!

4. And last but definitely not least, my **Reading Roadmap PD**. Yes, I'm a bit biased, but the training is truly unlike anything else available. The Reading Roadmap PD gives you the knowledge you need to be a

highly effective reading teacher as well as the tools necessary to immediately implement the strategies. All of the tools I mentioned in this list as well as assessments, decodable passages, decodable literacy centers, and so many more are included with this training.

SCAN ME

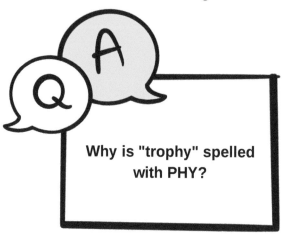

Why is "trophy" spelled with PHY?

I'm so glad you asked about this because I get similar questions all the time.

If you have wracked your brain trying to figure out what spelling patterns explain a specific word, my No. 1 tip is to do a Google search for its origin. In this case, *trophy* comes from Greek so the /f/ sound is spelled with *PH*. Other Greek-originating words that include that spelling are *photo* and *alphabet*.

Most English words are predictable, but words like this one almost seem out of place at first. A famous linguistic joke from the 1800s illustrates how nonsensical some spellings can be by suggesting that the word *fish* could be spelled in a new way: *ghoti* because if we used the gh from laugh, the o in women, and the ti in nation, and pronounced them the same way they are in their original words, the letters g-h-o-t-i would say "fish." #geekyhumor

The Science of Reading in Action

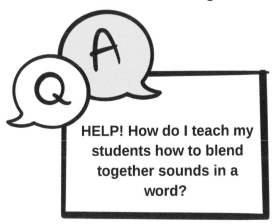

HELP! How do I teach my students how to blend together sounds in a word?

When it comes to blending, here are three of my favorite tips and tricks:

1. Practice with continuous sounds. When you are blending, it can help to practice with continuous sounds because they link smoothly into the next sound. These are all continuous sounds: /a/ /e/ /f/ /i/ /l/ /m/ /n/ /o/ /r/ /s/ /u/ /v/ /w/ /y/ /z/.

2. Try singing the sounds. When you sing the sounds in a word, you are forced to hold that sound until you slide into the next one. Whether you intend to or not, you will naturally blend the sounds. You don't need a tune, just hold one single note all the way through. Sing these words to try it out: sun, am, fin.

3. Make blending tactile. Hands-on tools can be really helpful for some learners. I love using rubber bands for blending. (Slinkies work well too!) Loop a rubber band around your middle fingers so you can stretch it apart each time you say a new sound like this:

/s/ (stretch)
/u/ (stretch)
/n/ (stretch)

Then clap your hands together as you blend the sounds to make the complete word: SUN (clap)

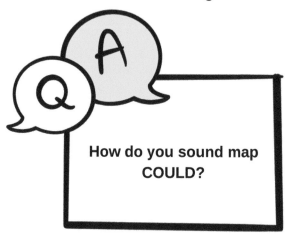

How do you sound map COULD?

I love seeing specific examples too! In fact, there's an entire training on sound mapping inside my Reading Roadmap training. To sound map could (or any word!), complete these six steps:

1. **Tap it**
2. **Map it**
3. **Graph it**
4. **Write it**
5. **Read it**
6. **Repeat steps 1–5 four more times**

Let's work through all of those steps together so that you know what they will look like.

1. Tap the sounds you hear with your fingers hitting the tabletop or the palm of your other hand: /c/ (tap) /ŏŏ/ (tap) /d/ (tap)
2. Map the sounds you hear by sliding a manipulative like a mini eraser or counting chip into each sound box as you say the sounds again: /c/ (slide) /ŏŏ/ (slide) /d/ (slide)
3. Graph the sounds by writing the letters used to spell each phoneme in the corresponding sound box as you say the sounds again: /c/ (write C) /ŏŏ/ (write OUL) /d/ (write D) **NOTE:** When L comes after the letters A, O, or U, it is often silent.
4. Write the complete word from start to finish as you say the sounds a fourth time: /c/ (write C) /ŏŏ/ (write OUL) /d/ (write D)

5. Read the word as you slide your finger underneath the letters from left to right: COULD

6. Repeat steps 1 to 5 four more times to help children memorize the word.

Scan the QR code to see me sound map the word could.

SCAN ME

After mapping could, ask students to map the words would and should to help them notice that the only difference between them is the beginning sound.

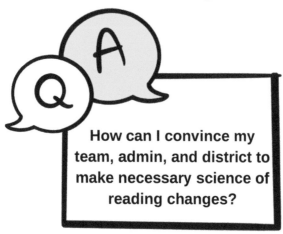

How can I convince my team, admin, and district to make necessary science of reading changes?

You asked the million-dollar question! Researchers, policymakers, and science of reading fans around the world are wondering that same thing too.

First, prove that using research-driven teaching strategies and tools improves students' reading growth by implementing them yourself. That might sound obvious, but there is so much power in data. When you can show the difference between student gains made without science-based teaching tools and strategies compared with your gains made with brain-friendly techniques, leaders will be more inclined to listen. It's hard to argue that the science of reading is a passing fad when there is so much proof for the significant positive impact it makes on students' reading scores.

Second, share this book with your administrators, department head, and colleagues. Equip your team to learn the history and research too. Because the science of reading consists of decades of brain scans, case studies, and reports, it can be hard to know where to start. This book cuts away the overwhelm and provides an easy-to-understand launching point.

Third, focus first on what is within your sphere of control. District-wide change often requires time, patience, and more reach than you may have. Although advocacy is extremely valuable, don't let it zap your energy or make you bitter. Focus most of your effort on improving the things you can control: your professional growth and best teaching practices. Momentum is contagious! When your students are flourishing, your colleagues will take notice. Soon they will be asking you to share your secrets so they can have that same success in their classrooms.

Call to Action

1. If you are on social media, I would love to become Insta-friends! Follow my feed @playdough2plato.

2. Send me a *Dm* so the SoR team and I can say "hello!"

Chapter Ten: What's Next?

You made it to the final chapter, and I could not be more impressed by your hard work and dedication. Let's pull out the party poppers and throw the confetti! Putting the science of reading into action takes a deep commitment to improving your teaching. You have learned so much! I hope that you have already implemented some of these strategies and have seen improvements in your students' reading.

Every teaching win, student success, and lightbulb moment you experience is a result of the choice you have made to learn and grow as an educator so your students could reach their fullest potential. The science of reading is not about reading ten chapters. It is about making lifelong learning a professional habit. And that is exactly what you are doing. Now that you have reached the final pages of this book, it is natural to wonder what is next.

First, continue putting the science of reading into action. You can go back to any of the videos or downloads whenever you need them. As you implement more of the teaching strategies included in these pages and QR codes, your confidence will grow right along with your teaching results. You will walk through school with your head held increasingly higher because you know, without a shadow of a doubt, you are doing everything in your power to help your students become thriving readers. The proof will be in your student test scores.

Don't be surprised if other teachers ask for your advice when they see your newfound success. You will become a leader not only in your classroom but also in your school, and your impact will begin to multiply. As you help other teachers implement the science of reading, they will become empowered to help their students too. As the old saying goes, we rise by lifting others.

Take It Further

Teaching reading does not have to be complicated; in fact, my primary goal is to make it easy for you to experience wildly successful results. I hope that our journey together is only at its beginning. I would love to have you join me inside The Reading Roadmap training so you can learn the four-step ACED system that makes it quick and easy to create highly tailored lessons based on each student's needs and strengths. Most alumni from the course report saving an average of two hours in lesson planning each week.

Many teachers think that to help their students learn reading faster, they just need to work harder. The truth is that teaching reading is not about working *harder*, it is about working *smarter.* As you know firsthand, if you do not use teaching tools and strategies that are based on proven research results, your lessons will be ineffective. And ineffective lessons keep you and your students stuck because your reading lessons only *kind of* work *some* of the time. Students will slip through the cracks, you'll get frustrated, and you'll continue to spend nights and weekends trying to piece together lesson plans that will fix it.

As you have already seen, there is an easier way! When you have research-based, classroom-tested teaching strategies and tools, everything changes. Your students have bigger, faster reading growth, and *you* gain unshakable teaching confidence. You can swap those time-consuming Google searches for Netflix shows and quality time with family and friends. And that nagging worry that some students are slipping through the cracks? It disappears forever because you know, without a doubt, that you are using the best teaching strategies.

Wherever you are on the science of reading journey, you have already taken the most important step by choosing to learn the brain-friendly practices that make it easier for children to read. Thank you for being here and diving into the research. I look forward to the day when we can look at students' assessment scores and see *all* children reading so they are empowered to reach their fullest potential. Good teaching changes families, communities, and the world.

All my love,

Malia

Call to Action

1. Share your favorite ah-ha moment or science of reading teaching win on social media to help spread the movement. **#scienceofreadinginaction**

2. Check out The Reading Roadmap PD to see whether it is a good next step for you!

To Book PD

SCAN ME

Appendix A
CONSONANT PHONEMES

Phoneme (Speech sound)	Grapheme (Letters used to spell it)	Examples
/b/	b, bb	bed, bubble
/d/	d, dd, ed	duck, add, pulled
/f/	f, ff, ph, gh	fin, photo, laugh
/g/	g, gg	get, egg
/h/	h	him
/j/	j, g, ge, dge	jet, gym, barge, budget
/k/	c, k, ck, ch, cc, que	cat, kite, back, school, occur, antique
/l/	l, ll	left, fill
/m/	m, mm, mb	make, hammer, crumb
/n/	n, nn, kn, gn	no, dinner, knob, gnome
/p/	p, pp	pig, hippo
/r/	r, rr, wr	robe, purr, write
/s/	s, se, ss, c, ce, sc	sat, house, fuss, city, mice, scissors
/t/	t, tt, ed	tin, letter, clapped
/v/	v, ve	van, have
/w/	w	will, swap
/y/	y, i	yes, billion
/z/	z, zz, ze, s, se, x	zoo, buzz, snooze, laser, was, hose, xylophone
/kw/	qu	queen
/ch/	ch, tch	chat, pitch
/sh/	sh, ss, ch, ti, ci	shop, mission, chef, nation, glacier

The Science of Reading in Action

Phoneme (Speech sound)	Grapheme (Letters used to spell it)	Examples
/th/ unvoiced	th	thank, thin, thing
/th/ voiced	th	then, that, feather
/ng/	ng, n	ring, monkey, rink
/zh/	ge, s	challenge, measure
/wh/ with breath	wh	what, why, when

VOWEL PHONEMES

	Phoneme (Speech sound)	Grapheme (Letters used to spell it)	Examples
Short Vowels	short /ă/	a, au	man, gauge
	short /ĕ/	e, ea	pen, head
	short /ĭ/	i	it
	short /ŏ/	o, a, au, aw, ough	dot, want, author, paw, fought
	short /ŭ/	u, o	up, ton
Long Vowels	long /ā/	a, a_e, ay, ai, ey, ei	bacon, cake, say, braid, they, eight
	long /ē/	e, e_e, ea, ee, ey, ie, y	he, these, meat, feet, key, chief, baby
	long /ī/	i, i_e, igh, y, ie	find, hide, sight, sky, pie
	long /ō/	o, o_e, oa, ou, ow, _oe	go, note, coat, soul, mow
	long /ū/	u, ue, u_e, ew	human, fuel, use, chew
Other Vowels	short /ŏŏ/	oo, u, oul	foot, put, should
	long /ōō/	oo, u, u_e, ui	room, truth, rule, fruit
Diphthong Vowels	/ow/ diphthong	ow, ou, ou_e	how, ouch, mouse
	/oy/ diphthong	oi, oy	oil, boy

The Science of Reading in Action

	Phoneme (Speech sound)	Grapheme (Letters used to spell it)	Examples
R-Influenced Vowels	short /ar/	ar	tar
	long /ar/	air, ear, are	hair, bear, dare
	/ir/	irr, ere, eer	mirror, here, deer
	/or/	or, ore, oor	or, more, door
	/ur/	ur, ir, er, ear, or, ar	hurt, bird, her, heard, work, dollar

Appendix B

The 7 Jobs of Silent E

1. A silent final E makes the vowel before it say its long sound: make, bite, pole, cube.
2. English words cannot end in the letters V or U, so E may be added: have, give, blue, clue.
3. A silent final E makes a C say /s/ and the G say /j/: face, ice, huge, age.
4. Every syllable must have a written vowel, so E is added when a syllable has just an L: little, turtle, waffle, google.
5. A silent E keeps singular words that end in S from being mistaken as plural: moose, purse, goose, house.
6. A silent E makes TH say its voiced sound: bath versus bathe, cloth versus clothe.
7. E is added to help distinguish between similar words: by versus bye, or versus ore.

Note: Sometimes an E is added for unknown reasons, as in done, come, were, where.

References

Chapter One

"The National Assessment of Education Progress (NAEP) tracks student achievement . . ."

National Assessment of Educational Progress. NAEP Nations Report Card.
  (2019). National Center for Education Statistics. 2019.
    https://nces.ed.gov/nationsreportcard/

"For instance, low literacy levels in adulthood lead to fewer employment opportunities and lower pay . . ."

"Program for the International Assessment for Adult Competencies
  (PIAAC)—U.S. State and County Estimates." *National Center for Education
  Statistics*. https://nces.ed.gov/surveys/piaac/state-county-estimates.asp

Rothwell, Jonathan. "Assessing the Economic Gains of Eradicating Illiteracy
  Nationally and Regionally in the United States." Barbara Bush Foundation
  for Family Literacy, 2020.

"It is not surprising that in 2017, the United States Department of Education confirmed income is strongly related to literacy . . ."

"Program for the International Assessment for Adult Competencies
  (PIAAC)—U.S. State and County Estimates." *National Center for Education
  Statistics*. https://nces.ed.gov/surveys/piaac/state-county-estimates.asp

"Research shows that a linguistically rich home environment is the most important contributing factor to children's early literacy and language development . . ."

Bus, Adriana G., Marinus H. Van Ijzendoorn, and Anthony D. Pellegrini. (1995). "Joint Book Reading Makes for Success in Learning to Read: A Meta-analysis on Intergenerational Transmission of Literacy."*Review of Educational Research,*65, no. 1 (1995): 1-21.

Logan, Jessica A. R., Laura M. Justice, Melike Yumus, and Leydi Johana Chaparro-Moreno. "When Children Are Not Read to at Home: The Million Word Gap."*Journal of Developmental & Behavioral Pediatrics,*40, no. 5 (2019): 383-386.

Moats, Louisa C., & Carol A. Tolman. *LETRS (*Volume1). Lexia Learning, 2019.

"Children who start school with an abundant word bank have a launching pad..."

Bryce, Nadine. "Meeting the Reading Challenges of Science Textbooks in the Primary Grades."*The Reading Teacher,*64, no. 7 (2011):474-485.

Gest, Scott D., Nicole R. Freeman, Celene E. Domitrovich, and Janet A. Welsh. (2004). "Shared Book Reading and Children's Language Comprehension Skills: The Moderating Role of Parental Discipline Practices." *Early Childhood Research Quarterly,*19, no. 2 (2004): 319-336.

U.S. Department of Health & Human Services. (2010, October 25). "Improving Mothers' Literacy Skills May Be the Best Way to Boost Children's Achievement." October 25, 2010. *National Institutes of Health.*

"When we add up the effects associated with low literacy levels, it is incredibly costly..."

"Why Literacy." (n.d.). *World Literacy Foundation.* Worldliteracyfoundation.org.

"Research shows that with the right tools and strategies, 95 percent of neurotypical students can learn to read by the end of first grade..."

Moats, Louisa C., & Carol A. Tolman. *LETRS* (Volume1). Lexia Learning, 2019.

"Narrowing the Third-Grade Reading Gap: Embracing the Science of Reading."
2019.*EAB.com; Educational Advisory Board.* https://eab.com/

"When humans experience stress or perceive danger, the brain sends a distress signal to the nervous system..."

Gray, Jeffrey A. *The Psychology of Fear and Stress,* Volume 5. CUP
Archive. 1987. New York, NY: McGraw-Hill.

McCarty, R. "The Fight-or-Flight Response: A Cornerstone of Stress Research."
Chapter 4, in *Stress: Concepts, Cognition, Emotion, and Behavior: Handbook of Stress Series Volume 1,*edited by George Fink. 2016. Cambridge, MA:
ScienceDirect; Academic Press.

"The history of reading wars..."

Chall, Jeanne S. *Learning to Read: The Great Debate.* Belmont, CA:
Wadsworth Publishing Company, 1995.

Gray, William S. *On Their Own in Reading: How to Give Children Independence in Analyzing New Words*. 1960. Northbrook, IL:Scott, Foresman and Co.

Flesch, Rudolf. *Why Johnny Can't Read: And What You Can Do About It*. 1986.New York: Harper and Brothers.

Hanford, E. (2018, September 10). *Why Aren't Kids Being Taught to Read?* Podcast audio. www.apmreports.org.

Kim, James S. "Research and the Reading Wars." *Phi Delta Kappa*, 89, no. 5 (2008): 372-375.

Moats, Louisa Cook, and Susan Brady. *Speech to Print: Language Essentials for Teachers*. Baltimore, MD: Brookes Publishing, 2020.

National Assessment of Educational Progress. NAEP Nations Report Card. (1994). National Center for Education Statistics. 2019. https://nces.ed.gov/nationsreportcard/

Pattan. "A Conversation with Emily Hanford: At a Loss for Words—Episode 9." 2019. *YouTube*. https://www.youtube.com/watch?v=hug2itzrflw

Smith, Frank. (2006). *Reading without Nonsense, 4th edition.*New York, NY: Teachers College Press; 2006.

"Sold a Story: How Teaching Kids to Read Went So Wrong." *APM Reports*. 2022. https://features.apmreports.org/sold-a-story/

U.S. Department of Health & Human Services. "Teaching Children to Read: An
Evidence-Based Assessment of Scientific Research Literature on Reading
and Its Implications for Reading Instruction." 2000. *National Reading Panel.*

WISE Channel. *How the Brain Learns to Read—Prof. Stanislas Dehaene*
[YouTube Video]. 2013. https://www.youtube.com/watch?v=25GI3-kiLdo

Chapter Two

*"Nancy Young, a dyslexia expert, created an image called the Ladder of
Reading…"*

Ladder of Reading Infographic. (n.d.). International Dyslexia Association.
https://dyslexiaida.org/ladder-of-reading-infographic-structured-literacy-helps-
all-students/

*"Picture cave dwellers communicating 100,000 years ago when we first
developed our anatomy for vocal tracts…"*

Wolf, Maryanne. *Proust and the Squid: The Story and Science of the Reading
Brain.*London: Icon Books, 2008.

Dehaene, Stanislas. *Reading in the Brain: The New Science of How We Read.*
London: Penguin Books, 2010.

WISE Channel. *How the Brain Learns to Read—Prof. Stanislas Dehaene*
[YouTube Video]. 2013. https://www.youtube.com/watch?v=25GI3-kiLdo

*"As I mentioned earlier, studies show that only 5 percent of students
can teach themselves how to read without support…"*

Hempenstall, Kerry, & Jennifer Buckingham. *Read About It: Scientific Evidence for Effective Teaching of Reading.*St Leonards, NSW:Centre for Independent Studies Limited, 2016.

U.S. Department of Health & Human Services. "Teaching Children to Read: An Evidence-Based Assessment of Scientific Research Literature on Reading and Its Implications for Reading Instruction." 2000.*National Reading Panel.*

"For decades, it was the backbone of popular programs, including Reading Recovery, Fountas and Pinnell, and Lucy Calkins' Units of Study..."

Geiger, Anna. Reaction to Fountas & Pinnell #2: Fountas & Pinnell are wrong about three-cueing.Podcast audio.The Measured Mom, 2021. https://www.themeasuredmom.com/reaction-to-fountas-pinnell-2-fountas-pinnell-are-wrong-about-three-cueing/

Goodman, Ken. "Reading Association." Originally Published in Journal of the *Reading Specialist,*6 (1967): 126-135.

Hanford, Emily, and Christopher Peak. "Influential authors Fountas and Pinnell stand behind disproven reading theory." 2021. *www.apmreports.org.*

Schwartz, Sarah. "Is This the End of "Three Cueing"? *Education Week.* December 16, 2020. https://www.edweek.org/teaching-learning/is-this-the-end-of-three-cueing/2020/12

"Sold a Story: How Teaching Kids to Read Went So Wrong." *APM Reports.* 2022. https://features.apmreports.org/sold-a-story/

"And yet, since the 1960s, classroom studies of reading methods have consistently shown better results for early phonics instruction..."

Nicholson, Tom. "Do Children Read Words Better in Context or in Lists? A Classic Study Revisited."*Journal of Educational Psychology,*83, no. 4 (1991): 444-450.

Rayner, Keith, Barbara R. Foorman, Charles A. Perfetti, David Pesetsky, and Mark S. Seidenberg. (2001). "How Psychological Science Informs the Teaching of Reading." *Psychological Science in the Public Interest,*2, no. 2 (2001): 31-74.

"It is a game. In fact, Ken Goodman, one of the creators of the three-cueing system, famously called it just that..."

Goodman, Ken. "Reading: A Psycholinguistic GuessingGame." *Journal of the Reading Specialist,*6, no. 4 (1976): 126-135.

"Australia's 2005 report Teaching of Literacy explains..."

Rose, Jim. Independent Review of the Teaching of Early Reading (UK)—The Rose Report.*Department for Education and Skills,*2006. https://dera.ioe.ac.uk/5551/2/report.pdf

"After your eyes scan the page to pull out letter chunks . . ."

Dehaene, Stanislaus. Reading in the Brain: The New Science of How We Read. London: Penguin Books, 2010.

Moats, Louisa C., and Carol A. Tolman. *LETRS* (Volume1). Lexia Learning, 2019.

"Professor and researcher David Kilpatrick explains . . ."

Kilpatrick, David A. Equipped for Reading Success: *A Comprehensive, Step-By-Step Program for Developing Phonemic Awareness and Fluent Word Recognition.Cicero, NY:Casey & Kirsch Publishers, 2016.*

"But research has proven that those audio stories absolutely count and the benefits are extensive . . ."

Baskin, Barbara H., & Karen Harris. (1995). "Heard Any Good Books Lately? The Case for Audiobooks in the Secondary Classroom."*Journal of Reading*, 38, no. 5 (1995): 372-376.

Cunningham, Anne, and David Rose. "This Is Your Brain on Reading: Knowledge Acquisition and Reading." 2013.*Scholastic.*

"First, let's look at the Simple View of Reading . . ."

Gough, Philip B., and William E. Tunmer. "Decoding, Reading, and Reading Disability."*Remedial and Special Education*, 7, no.1 (1986): 6-10.

"This bucket does not refer to a child's ability to comprehend what they are reading. Reading comprehension comes later . . ."

Baker, Scott K., R. T. Santiago, J. Masser, N. J. Nelson, and J. Turtura. "The Alphabetic Principle: From Phonological Awareness to Reading Words." Improving Literacy Brief.*National Center on Improving Literacy*, 2018.

Birner, Betty. "FAQ: Language Acquisition." *LinguisticSociety of America*, 2012

Byrne, Brian, and Ruth Fielding-Barnsley. "Phonemic Awareness and Letter

   Knowledge in the Child's Acquisition of the Alphabetic Principal." *Journal*

   of Educational Psychology, 81, no. 3 (1989): 313-321.

Ehri, Linnea C. (1991). "Development in the Ability to Read Words." In *Handbook*

   of Reading Research, Volume II, edited by RebeccaBarr, Michael L Kamil,

   Peter B. Mosenthal, & P. David Pearson, 383-417.

Moats, Louisa C., and Carol A. Tolman. *LETRS* (Volume1). Lexia Learning,
   2019.

**"It does not matter how much background knowledge she has on solar
panels . . ."**

Kang, Eun Young, and Mikyung Shin. "The Contributions of Reading Fluency and

   Decoding to Reading Comprehension for Struggling Readers in Fourth

   Grade." *Reading & Writing Quarterly,*35, no. 3 (2019),179-192.

Speece, Deborah L., Kristen D. Ritchey, Rebecca Silverman, Christopher

   Schatschneider, Caroline Y. Walker, and Katryna N. Andrusik. (2010).

   "Identifying Children in Middle Childhood Who Are at Risk for Reading

   Problems."*School Psychology Review*, 39, no. 2 (2010):258-276.

**"As this example illustrates, even with the most amazing word-reading
ability, if students have zero language comprehension, they also have
zero reading comprehension . . ."**

Braze, David, Whitney Tabor, Donald P. Shankweiler, and W. Einar Mencl.

   "Speaking Up for Vocabulary: Reading Skill Differences in Young Adults."

   Journal of Learning Disabilities 40, no. 3 (2007):226-243.

Cain, Kate, Jane V. Oakhill, Marcia A. Barnes, and Peter E. Bryant.

"Comprehension Skill, Inference-Making Ability, and Their Relation to

Knowledge."*Memory & Cognition*29, no. 6 (2001): 850-859.

Catts, Hugh W., Suzanne M. Adlof, and Susan E. Weismer. (2006). "Language

Deficits in Poor Comprehenders: A Case for the Simple View of Reading."

Journal of Speech, Language, and Hearing Research,49, no. 2 (2006):

278-293.

Catts, Hugh W., Marc E. Fey, Xuyang Zhang, & J. Bruce Tomblin. (1999).

"Language Basis of Reading and Reading Disabilities: Evidence from a

Longitudinal Investigation. "*Scientific Studies of Reading*, 3, no. 4 (1999):

331-361.

Echeverri Acosta, Luz Marina, & McNulty Ferri, Maria. (2010). "Reading Strategies

to Develop Higher Thinking Skills for Reading Comprehension. "*Profile Issues

in Teachers Professional Development,*12, no. 1 (2010):107-123.

International Dyslexia Association. "Scarborough's Reading Rope: A

Groundbreaking Infographic—International Dyslexia Association." April 2,

2018. Dyslexiaida.org.

Lonigan, Christopher J., Stephen R. Burgess, and Christopher

Schatschneider."Examining the Simple View of Reading with Elementary School

Children: Still Simple After All These Years." *Remedial and SpecialEducation*, 39,

no. 5 (2018): 260-273.

O'Reilly, Tenaha Zuowei Wang, and John Sabatini. "How Much Knowledge Is Too

Little? When a Lack of Knowledge Becomes a Barrier to Comprehension."

Psychological Science, 30, no. 9 (2019): 1344-1351.

"Research has proven that deliberate practice is key to evolving from novice to an expert. . ."

Brabeck, Mary, Jill Jeffrey, and Sara Fry. Practice for Knowledge Acquisition (Not Drill and Kill): Applications of Psychological Science to Teaching and Learning Modules. *American Psychological Association*, 2010.

Ericsson, K. Anders, Ralf Th. Krampe, and Clemens Tesch-Römer. "The Role of Deliberate Practice in the Acquisition of Expert Performance." *Psychological Review*, 100, no. 3 (1993): 363-406.

Chapter Three

"For decades, research has identified phonological awareness as a critical key to unlocking students' reading growth . . ."

Heggerty, Michael. *Phonemic Awareness: Primary Curriculum.* Literacy Resources, Incorporated, 2020.

Kilpatrick, David A. *Equipped for Reading Success:A Comprehensive, Step-by-Step Program for Developing Phonemic Awareness and Fluent Word Recognition.* Cicero, NY: Casey & Kirsch Publishers, 2016.

U.S. Department of Health and Human Services. "Teaching Children to Read: An Evidence-Based Assessment of Scientific Research Literature on Reading and Its Implications for Reading Instruction." 2000. *National Reading Panel.*

"When the National Reading Panel published its 2000 report, it identified more than 50 "gold standard" studies verifying it was a critical component of effective reading and spelling instruction . . ."

Kjeldsen, Ann-Christina, Antti Kärnä, Pekka Niemi, Åke Olofsson, and Katarina Witting. "Gains from Training in Phonological Awareness in Kindergarten Predict Reading Comprehension in Grade 9."*Scientific Studies of Reading*, 18, no. 6 (2014): 452-467.

Griffith, Priscilla L., and Mary W. Olson. "Phonemic Awareness Helps Beginning Readers Break the Code. "*The Reading Teacher*, 45,no. 7 (1992): 516-523.

Stanovich, Keith E., Anne E. Cunningham, and Barbara B. Cramer. "Assessing Phonological Awareness in Kindergarten Children: Issues of Task Comparability. "*Journal of Experimental Child Psychology*, 38, no. 2 (1984): 175-190.

Stanovich, Keith E. "Speculations on the Causes and Consequences of Individual Differences in Early Reading Acquisition" (pp 307-342)."*In Reading Acquisition,* edited by P. B. Gough, L. C. Ehri, andR. Treiman. Lawrence Erlbaum Associates, Inc., 2017.

U.S. Department of Health and Human Services. "Teaching Children to Read: An Evidence-Based Assessment of Scientific Research Literature on Reading and Its Implications for Reading Instruction." 2000. *National Reading Panel.*

"David Kilpatrick explains, "Every point in a child's development of word-level reading is substantially affected by phonological awareness . . ."

Kilpatrick, David A. *Equipped for Reading Success: A Comprehensive, Step-By-Step Program for Developing Phonemic Awareness and Fluent Word Recognition.* Cicero, NY:Casey & Kirsch Publishers, 2016.

"Because weak phonemic awareness is the most common factor in struggling readers' difficulties, analyzing it is absolutely crucial . . ."

Adams, Marilyn Jager. Beginning to Read: Thinking and Learning about Print. Baltimore, MD: Bradford Books, 1994.

Kilpatrick, David A. *Equipped for Reading Success:A Comprehensive, Step-By-Step Program for Developing Phonemic Awareness and Fluent Word Recognition.*Cicero, NY:Casey & Kirsch Publishers, 2016.

"These skills are presented in order from least to most difficult so you can picture how they build on one another..."

Brady, Susan. "*A 2020 perspective on research findings on alphabetics (phoneme awareness and phonics)*: Implications for instruction." The Reading League Journal, 2020.

Geiger, Anna. What we know about phoneme awareness with Dr. Susan Brady. Podcast audio. The Measured Mom, 2023. https://www.themeasuredmom.com/phoneme-awareness-susan-brady/

International Dyslexia Association. "Building Phoneme Awareness: Know What Matters." 2022. Dyslexiaida.org.

"Although you may not have noticed it before, spoken language is essentially a long string of sounds . . ."

Moats, Louisa Cook, and Susan Brady. *Speech to Print: Language Essentials for Teachers.* Brookes Publishing, 2020.

"Although English has only six letters—A, E,I, O, U, and sometimes Y —there are fifteen different vowels..."

Moats, Louisa C., and Carol A. Tolman. *LETRS* (Volume1). Lexia Learning, 2019.

Moats, Louisa Cook, and Susan Brady. *Speech to Print: Language Essentials for Teachers.*Brookes Publishing, 2020.

"Based on the Total Physical Response or TPR teaching method..."

Asher, James J. (1966). "The Learning Strategy of the Total Physical Response: A Review."*The Modern Language Journal,*50, no. 2 (1966):79-84.

"The first phonemic awareness skill students' brains are ready to tackle is blending phonemes..."

Moats, Louisa C., and Carol A. Tolman. *LETRS* (Volume1). Lexia Learning, 2019.

Paulson, Lucy Hart.*The Development of Phonological Awareness Skills in Preschool Children: From Syllables to Phonemes. 2004.* Graduate Student Theses, Dissertations, & Professional Papers. 9522. *https://scholarworks.umt.edu/etd/9522*

"Students' brains are first able to identify beginning sounds..."

Kilpatrick, David A. Equipped for Reading Success: A Comprehensive, Step-by-Step Program for Developing Phonemic Awareness and Fluent Word Recognition. Cicero, NY:Casey & Kirsch Publishers,2016.

"Bonus Fact:The Yale Center for Dyslexia and Creativity reports dyslexia is "very common, affecting 20 percent of the population . . ."

Catts, Hugh W., Marc E. Fey, Xuyang Zhang, and J. Bruce Tomblin. (1999). "Language Basis of Reading and Reading Disabilities: Evidence from a Longitudinal Investigation. "*Scientific Studies of Reading*, 3, no. 4 (1999): 331-361.

Jenkins, Joseph R., and Rollanda E. O'Connor. "Early Identification and Intervention for Young Children with Reading/Learning Disabilities." In *Identification of Learning Disabilities: Research to Practice*, edited by R. Bradley, L. Danielson, and D. P. Hallahan (pp. 99–149). Mahwah, NJ: Lawrence Erlbaum Associates Publishers, 2002.

Ozernov-Palchik, Ola, Elizabeth S. Norton, Georgios Sideridis, Sara D. Beach, Maryanne Wolf, John D. E. Gabrieli, and Nadine Gaab. "Longitudinal Stability of Pre-reading Skill Profiles of Kindergarten Children: Implications for Early Screening and Theories of Reading." *Developmental Science*, 20, no. 5 (2016): e12471.

Yale Center for Dyslexia & Creativity. (n.d.). "What Is Dyslexia?" https://dyslexia.yale.edu/dyslexia/what-is-dyslexia/

Chapter Four

"We can use thirty-one different phonics and spelling rules to explain between 96 and 98 percent of English words..."

Eide, Denise. *Uncovering the Logic of English: A Common-Sense Approach to Reading, Spelling, and Literacy.* Logic of English, Inc., 2012.

"Researcher Linnea Ehri's analysis of thirty-eightphonics studies explains..."

Ehri, Linnea C. "Systematic Phonics Instruction: Findings of the National Reading
    Panel." 2019. https://eric.ed.gov/?id=ED479646.

"Multisensory learning has proven benefits because it engages multiple areas of the brain at the same time...."

Başar, Errol. "The Theory of the Whole-Brain-Work." *International Journal of
    Psychophysiology,*60, no. 2 (2006): 133-138.

Blomert, Leo, and Dries Froyen. "Multi-sensory Learning and Learning to Read.
    *International Journal of Psychophysiology,*77, no.3 (2010): 195-204.

Fraga González, Goka, Gojko Žarić, Jurgen Tijms, Milene Bonte, and Moritz W.
    van der Molen. "Contributions of Letter-Speech Sound Learning and Visual
    Print Tuning to Reading Improvement: Evidence from Brain Potential and
    Dyslexia Training Studies."*Brain Sciences*, 7, no.12 (2017), 10.

Minnesota Literacy Council. "Multisensory Activities to Teach Reading Skills." 2015.
    https://www.literacymn.org/sites/default/files/multisensory_techniques_to_teach_
    reading_skills.pdf.

Sams, M., R. Aulanko, M. Hämäläinen, R. Hari, O. V. Lounasmaa, S.-T. Lu, and
    J. Simola, J. (1991). "Seeing Speech: Visual Information from Lip Movements
    Modifies Activity in the Human Auditory Cortex.*NeuroscienceLetters,*127, no. 1
    (1991): 141-145.

Shams, Ladan, and Aaron R. Seitz. (2008). "Benefits of Multisensory Learning."

Trends in Cognitive Sciences, 12, no. 11 (2008): 411-417.

"Investigating the look and feel of a phoneme is a helpful first step because it launches the learning from children's spoken language superpower...."

Moats, Louisa Cook, and Susan Brady. Speech to Print: Language

Essentials for Teachers.Brookes Publishing, 2020.

Moats, Louisa C., and Carol A. Tolman. LETRS (Volume1). Lexia Learning,
2019.

"Research shows that practicing spelling patterns within words (rather than as isolated rules) helps children learn more quickly and deeply..."

Ehri, Linnea C. "Systematic Phonics Instruction: Findings of the National Reading

Panel." 2019. https://eric.ed.gov/?id=ED479646.

Foorman, Barbara R., David J. Francis, Diana M. Novy, and Dov Liberman. "How

Letter-Sound Instruction Mediates Progress in First-Grade Reading and

Spelling." Journal of Educational Psychology,83,no. 4 (1991): 456-469.

Foorman, Barbara R., David J. Francis, Jack M. Fletcher, Christopher

Schatschneider, and Paras Mehta. "The Role of Instruction in Learning to

Read: Preventing Reading Failure in At-Risk Children." Journal of Educational

Psychology, 90, no. 1 (1998): 37-55.

Fulwiler, Gwen, and Patrick Groff. "The Effectiveness of Intensive Phonics."

Reading Horizons: A Journal of Literacy and Language Arts.21, no. 1

(1980).

Lum, T., and L. L. Morton. (1984). "Direct Instruction in Spelling Increases Gain in

Spelling and Reading Skills." Special Education in Canada,58, no. 2 (1984):

41-45.

Snider, Vicki E. (1990). "Direct Instruction Reading with Average First-Graders."

Reading Improvement, 27, no. 2 (1990): 143-148.

"After analyzing the phoneme and identifying words that include it, the next step is connecting the sound to the spellings. Research has proven that the majority of children require an explicit explanation to make that connection..."

Blevins, Wiley. Phonics from A to Z. Scholastic Teaching Resources, 2017.

Ehri, Linnea C. "Grapheme-Phoneme Knowledge Is Essential to Learning to

Read Words in English," in Word Recognition in Beginning Literacy, edited

by Jamie L. Metsala and Linnea C. Ehri. Oxfordshire, England: Routledge,

1998.

The schwa /ə/ in the middle of Vowel Valley is sometimes referred to as the "lazy vowel"..."

Skating Through Literacy (blog). (July 30, 2021). "How to Start Using a Vowel

Valley Sound Wall in Your Classroom."

https://www.skatingthroughliteracy.com/how-to-start-using-a-vowel-valley-

sound- wall-in-your-classroom/.

"There are dozens of different opinions about the best order to teach consonant sounds but no conclusive research exists...."

Ehri, Linnea C. "Systematic Phonics Instruction: Findings of the National Reading Panel." 2019. https://eric.ed.gov/?id=ED479646.

Moats, Louisa C. "Teaching Decoding." 1998. https://www.aft.org/ae/springsummer1998/moats.

"Basic Phonograms Chart..."

Eide, Denise. *Uncovering the Logic of English: A Common-Sense Approach t Reading, Spelling, and Literacy.*Logic of English,Inc., 2012.

Reithaug, Dawn. Orchestrating Success in Reading .Stirling Head Enterprises, 2002.

Chapter Five

"Humans simply do not have enough mental storage space to collect pictures of the millions of different ways every word might look..."

Dehaene, Stanislas. *Reading in the Brain: The New Science of How We Read.* London: Penguin Books, 2010.

Kilpatrick, David A. *Essentials of Assessing, Preventing,and Overcoming Reading Difficulties (Essentials of Psychological Assessment).*Hoboken, NJ: Wiley, 2015.

Kilpatrick, David A.*Equipped for Reading Success:A Comprehensive, Step-By-Step Program for Developing Phonemic Awareness and Fluent Word Recognition.*Cicero, NY:Casey & Kirsch Publishers, 2016.

"The steps are simple to implement, but the impact is significant. Good readers can memorize a new word in just one to five exposures when they connect a word's spelling, pronunciation, and meaning in one ready-to-retrieve mental file folder..."

Ehri, Linnea C. (2014) "Orthographic Mapping in the Acquisition of Sight Word Reading, Spelling Memory, and Vocabulary Learning," in *Scientific Studies of Reading*, 18, no. 1 (2014), 5-21, doi:10.1080/10888438.2013.819356

Kilpatrick, David A. *Equipped for Reading Success: A Comprehensive, Step-By-Step Program for Developing Phonemic Awareness and Fluent Word Recognition.* Cicero, NY: Casey & Kirsch Publishers,2016.

"When children begin memorizing sight words, they move through four distinct phases of development . . ."

Ehri, Linnea C. "Development of Sight Word Reading: Phases and Findings," (pp. 135–154) in **The Science of Reading: A Handbook** ,edited by M. J. Snowling & C. Hulme. 2005. Blackwell Publishing. https://doi.org/10.1002/9780470757642.ch8.

Kilpatrick, David A .*Equipped for Reading Success: A Comprehensive, Step-By-Step Program for Developing Phonemic Awareness and Fluent Word Recognition.*Cicero, NY:Casey & Kirsch Publishers,2016.

Chapter Six

"While there are an estimated 600,000 words in the English language, a 2019 survey found that just thirteen account for 25 percent of all the words in text . . ."

Johns, Jerry L., and Kristine H. Wilke. (2018). "High Frequency Words: Some Ways to Teach and Help Students Practice and Learn Them."*Texas Journal of Literacy Education,*6, no. 1 (2018), 3-13.

"David Kilpatrick explains that helping children connect pronunciation, spelling, and meaning instead of relying on inefficient visual memory makes it possible for them to memorize a word in just one to five exposures . . ."

Kilpatrick, David A. *Equipped for Reading Success:A Comprehensive, Step-By-Step Program for Developing Phonemic Awareness and Fluent Word Recognition.* Cicero, NY: Casey & Kirsch Publishers, 2016.

"When Linnea Ehri shared findings from the National Reading Panel in 2003, she highlighted..."

Ehri, Linnea C. "Systematic Phonics Instruction: Findings of the National Reading Panel." 2019. https://eric.ed.gov/?id=ED479646.

Chapter Seven

"Language comprehension is what makes stories enjoyable and books like this one educational. It involves three different brain tasks..."

Mann, Virginia A.*Theory and Practice of Early Reading,*Volume 2, edited by
Lauren B. Resnick and Phyllis B. Weaver. Hillsdale, NJ: Lawrence Erlbaum
Associates, 1979, p. 353.*Applied Psycholinguistics,*2, no. 3 (1981): 285-287.

Moats, Louisa C., and Carol A. Tolman. *LETRS* (Volume1). Lexia Learning, 2019.

Vellutino, Frank R., William E. Tunmer, James J. Jaccard, and RuSan Chen.
"Components of Reading Ability: Multivariate Evidence for a Convergent Skills
Model of Reading Development."*Scientific Studiesof Reading,*11, no. 1 (2007):
3-32.

Seidenberg, Mark S., and James L. McClelland. "A Distributed, Developmental
Model of Word Recognition and Naming."*PsychologicalReview,*96, no. 4
(1989): 523-568.

Seidenberg, Mark S. "The Science of Reading and Its Educational Implications."
Language Learning and Development, 9, no. 4 (2013):331-360.

"Language comprehension also involves..."

Dehaene, Stanislas. *Reading in the Brain: The New Science of How
We Read.* London: Penguin Books, 2010.

Moats, Louisa C., and Carol A. Tolman. LETRS (Volume 1). Lexia Learning,
2019.

"Because spoken language is a human superpower . . ."

Dehaene, Stanislas. *Reading in the Brain: The New Science of How We Read.*
London: Penguin Books, 2010.

Chapter Eight

"The LETRS training explains, "Language facility gained in earlier grades will have a major impact on reading comprehension . . ."

Moats, Louisa C., and Carol A. Tolman. *LETRS* (Volume 1). Lexia Learning,
2019.

Moats, Louisa C., and Carol A. Tolman. *LETRS* (Volume 2). Lexia Learning,
2019.

"Historically, classroom observations found that reading comprehension skills were assessed but rarely taught . . ."

Durkin, Dolores. "What Classroom Observations Reveal About Reading
Comprehension Instruction." *Reading Research Quarterly,*14, no. 4 (1978):
481-533.

"Today, however, we can draw on decades of scientific research that pinpoints the specific strategies that correspond to strong reading comprehension . . ."

Anderson, Richard C., and P. David Pearson. "A Schema-theoretic View of Basic Processes in Reading Comprehension" (pp. 255-291), in *Handbook of Reading Research, edited by* P. David Pearson, R. Barr, M. L. Kamil, and P. Mosenthal. 1984. New York: Longman, Inc.

Kintsch, Walter, and Tuen A. van Dijk. "Toward a Model of Text Comprehension and Production."*Psychological Review,*85, no. 5 (1978):363-394.

Pearson, P. David, and Margaret C. Gallagher. (1983). "The Instruction of Reading Comprehension." *Contemporary Educational Psychology,*8, no. 3 (1983): 317-344.

"In their review of comprehension research studies, David Pearson and Margaret Gallagher summarize . . ."

Pearson, P. David, and Margaret C. Gallagher. (1983). "The Instruction of Reading Comprehension." *Contemporary Educational Psychology,*8, no. 3 (1983): 317-344.

Additional Helpful Resources

Braze, David, Leonard Katz, James S. Magnuson, W. Einar Mencl, Whitney Tabor, Julie A. Van Dyke, Tao Gong, Clinton L. Johns, and Donald P. Shankweiler. "Vocabulary Does Not Complicate the Simple View of Reading. "*Reading and Writing,*29, no. 3 (2015): 435-451.

Castles, Anne, Kathleen Rastle, and Kate Nation. (2018). "Ending the Reading Wars: Reading Acquisition from Novice to Expert." Psychological Science in *the Public Interest,*19, no. 1 (2018): 5-51.

Catts, Hugh W., Donald Compton, J. Bruce Tomblin, and Mindy Sittner Bridges. (2012). "Prevalence and Nature of Late-Emerging Poor Readers." Journal of *Educational Psychology*, 104, no. 1 (2012): 166.

International Dyslexia Association. Multisensory Structured Language Teaching Fact Sheet. Retrieved from dyslexiaida.org: https://dyslexiaida.org/multisensory-structured-language-teaching-fact-sheet/

"Specific Learning Disability and SLD—Dyslexia." 2015. Stracener, Ashly. https://portal.ct.gov/SDE/Special-Education/Specific-Learning-Disability-and-SLD —Dyslexia.

Reading between the Lines: Exploring Literacy, The Science of Reading, and the RISE Initiative 2020. Scholars Day Conference. 10. https://scholarlycommons.obu.edu/scholars_day_conference/2020/ honors_th eses/10

Malia Hollowell is the founder and CEO of The Reading Roadmap, a revolutionary professional development training that provides the tools, training, and support teachers need to help every reader thrive. Malia is a National Board Certified teacher and earned her Master's in Education from Stanford University. She and her husband live just outside of Seattle, Washington, with their three children. You can connect with her on Instagram at @playdough2plato.

Bring the Science of Reading to Your School or District.

Thanks to decades of research, brain scans, and case studies, scientists have pinpointed how brains learn to read. They know what tools and strategies work and (more importantly) what does not work so every student can experience significant reading growth.

But until now, that information has not been easily accessible to the people who need it most: the educators who are actually teaching children to read. Malia Hollowell's professional development changes that by giving teachers the knowledge, tools, and strategies they need to confidently put the science of reading into action in their twenty-first century classrooms.

Malia's highly engaging trainings empower teachers to:

- Understand how students learn to read on a scientific, research-based level so they can do more of what works and less of what doesn't
- Build students' phonological awareness and phonics skills so they have a rock-solid foundation that propels reading growth
- Confidently differentiate for a variety of student learning needs and strengths - even in very diverse classrooms
- Become leaders in their organization who work collaboratively to problem solve learning challenges and accelerate every students' reading growth

The Reading Roadmap Course

The Reading Roadmap Course is in a category of its own because it pairs must-know training about how brains learn to read with the research-based tools and strategies teachers need to actually implement the learning in their classrooms. The cutting-edge professional development goes beyond traditional teacher training by providing a proven teaching system for getting significant reading results.

In just 4 short weeks, you will:

- Have a rock-solid understanding of what the research does (and does not!) tell us about how students learn to read.
- Use quick, 5-minute assessments to uncover what your students are really struggling with so you can fill hidden holes that are keeping them stuck
- Implement simple, research-based teaching strategies and tools that help students learn to read 10 x faster
- Learn when to teach specific phonics skills so you understand the step-by-step process from start to finish
- Use done-for-you lesson plans and centers that save you valuable planning and prep time

CHECK OUT MORE FROM TEACHERGOALS PUBLISHING!

MONSTERS HAVE MANNERS
BY JEFF KUBIAK

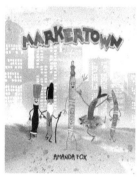

MARKERTOWN
BY AMANDA FOX

PETER O' METER
BY TRICIA FUGLESTAD

THE SNOW FLURRY FAIRY
BY TRICIA FUGLESTAD

Purchase signed copies of our children's books, book virtual readings, or buy in bulk for your school by going to the link below or scanning the QR code!

For more information go to:
https://teachergoals.com/books/childrens-books/

MY FIRST AUGMENTED REALITY Workbook Series

Learning fundamental writing and math skills has never been more engaging than our My First Augmented Reality Workbook Series. Using the Quiver app, students will unlock interactive experiences that will teach path of motion, phonics, writing, and more! This is great for schools that are 1:1 or have tablet stations set up for students to learn.

TeacherGoals Publishing is an educational publishing company that is set on disrupting the way kids learn, read, and develop literacy and math skills. Our books and workbooks come enhanced with augmented reality. Augmented reality overlays digital content and information onto the physical world, in this instance, digital content that explains, instructs, and even guides students through skill-building. Kids can unlock this content by downloading the Quiver app and scanning the pages. When scanned, the pages come to life and leave kids wanting to revisit the workbooks again and again. Email us about bulk purchases for your classroom, school, or district today!

- Requires download of the free Quiver App.
- Quiver Subscription is needed to enjoy Augmented Reality content.
- Suitable on Android and Apple smart devices such as phones or tablets.
- Includes interactive augmented reality scenes.

Email us for special pricing on bulk purchases for your classroom, school, or district.

publishing@teachergoals.com

www.teachergoals.com/bulk

More From TeacherGoals

THE AI CLASSROOM
DAN FITZPATRICK, AMANDA FOX, & BRAD WEINSTEIN

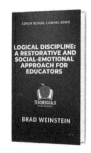

LOGICAL DISCIPLINE
BY BRAD WEINSTEIN, NATHAN MAYNARD, AND DR. LUKE ROBERTS

HEARTLEADER
BY MATTHEW J. BOWERMAN

THE CANVA MATH CLASSROOM
HEATHER BROWN AND AMANDA FOX

THE CANVA CLASSROOM
AMANDA FOX

THE CANVA SCHOOL
DR. JOHN WICK & DANAE ACKER

THE CANVA SOCIAL STUDIES CLASSROOM
KATHERINE GOYETTE & ADAM JUAREZ

THE A TO Z FIELD GUIDE TO CANVA
AMANDA FOX